KINGDOM COME

David Wright

I John 2:6

KINGDOM COME

IN MY LIFE, IN THE CHURCH, IN THE WORLD

DAVID WRAIGHT

YFCIM Publishing
7670 S Vaughn Ct.
Englewood, CO 80112
www.yfci.org
© David Wraight 2011

Produced with the assistance of The Livingstone Corporation (www.LivingstoneCorp.com).
Project staff includes Dave Veerman, Linda Taylor, Larry Taylor, Tom Freking, Andy Culbertson,
and Cheryl Dunlop.

To my wife Jenny

. . . for her unending love, support and partnership in this exciting and challenging life that God has called us to.

TABLE OF CONTENTS

ACKNOWLEDGMENTS

After writing my first book, *The Next Wave*, I was not keen to write another. Although I enjoy writing and the end product of my first effort has been used to encourage and inspire others, it is an onerous task, particularly in the context of the demands of my current ministry leadership role. However, with the encouragement of my family, friends and ministry colleagues I ventured out once more into the realm of authorship. Without their support this book would not have been written.

Many helped in the editing and refining of the manuscript: my wife, Jenny, who spent hours reading and re-reading text and sat beside me as we worked together through the whole manuscript; my parents, Malcolm and Val Wraight, whose affirmation and helpful comments motivated me to "get it right"; Robert Freeman, who on very short notice waded through the first draft refining and improving the text; and my friends and colleagues who provided invaluable insight, input and counsel on the material and concepts covered in the book.

I am extremely grateful for the Youth for Christ team who created the space for me to write. They willingly took up the slack created by my absence and encouraged me along the way, sustaining me with their prayers and words of affirmation.

I would also like to acknowledge my ministry partners at

Livingstone who were prepared to step up and do all that was required to get this book published in a short time frame.

And finally, I wish to acknowledge my Lord and Savior Jesus Christ, who loves me and all the people of this world with an unimaginable love and calls us to "make disciples of all nations" by living as authentic followers of him in a world that is longing for the Kingdom to come.

ABOUT THE AUTHOR

After leaving promising careers in horticultural science and early childhood education, David Wraight and his wife, Jenny, commenced their ministry life in their early twenties serving in an Aboriginal community in Western Australia and caring for neglected and abused Aboriginal children. Following their time in Western Australia, David served as a pastor and youth counsellor at a church in Melbourne, Australia, developing an extensive youth ministry, including an innovative youth accommodation and counselling program. In 1990 David joined Youth for Christ (YFC), initially serving as Executive Director of YFC Melbourne and then as National Director of YFC Australia. For five years he served as the YFC Asia Pacific Area Director until being appointed to his current role of International President/CEO.

David and Jenny have three children—Belinda, Tracey and Michael—and currently live in Denver, Colorado, the location of YFC International's headquarters.

To contact David or to learn more about him and his ministry, visit his Web site: www.davidwraight.com.

INTRODUCTION

*. . . your kingdom come, your will be done
on earth as it is in heaven.*

(Matthew 6:10)

The music throbbed. The band could be felt as much as heard as the huge subs on the edge of the stage transmitted a deep bass resonance that felt like it was rearranging the organs in your body. Screaming guitars, clouds of CO_2 "smoke" and spinning multicolored lights added to the experience. The young people loved it!

It was the first night of our Live Band Coffee Shop. I was a young pastor serving in a church in the southeastern suburbs of Melbourne. The young people of the church were keen to reach their friends and had come up with the idea that to do this effectively they needed to create an environment that would be attractive and culturally relevant. They figured that getting their friends to come to church was a pretty challenging proposition, as many of their peers had never been in a church before and largely viewed Christians as an insular and out-of-touch bunch of weirdoes. So we rented a local community hall and set up the venue with candlelit tables, subdued lighting, a dance area and a stage for the bands.

The invitations went out, sound equipment and lighting were bought or hired, Christian bands were booked, advertising was placed in local newspapers, and the first night had arrived.

Ministry Dilemmas

The evening started off slowly with only a few extra young people turning up besides the youth of the church. I started to worry if this whole venture was going to work. But as the night progressed more and more young people arrived. It wasn't long before the place was packed.

The idea was that the youth of the church would mix with the young people attending the event, engage in conversations over soda and coffee and build relationships that would eventually provide opportunity to share Jesus and connect unchurched young people to the church community. As the band started up, I enthusiastically mixed with the crowd, endeavoring to strike up meaningful conversations with young people on the dance floor or at the tables.

It wasn't long before I realized that we had a significant flaw in our strategy. With the band belting out their numbers at exceptionally high but culturally mandated decibels, the only possible way of verbally communicating with anyone was to yell at the top of your voice a couple of inches from their ear! I persisted, yelling at people for about an hour, but eventually gave up, realizing that all I was achieving was significant damage to my voice and my hearing.

Thinking this relational building strategy was a dismal failure, I decided I needed to get free of the noise for a while to try to work out what could be done to rescue the whole venture. With ears ringing and hissing I exited the building, only to find a crowd of young people congregated around the entrance to the hall, many of them freely chatting with members of our youth outreach team. It was there that I met

Julie.[1] She was standing on the edge of the crowd by herself. I walked over to her and introduced myself, asked her name and started chatting to her about her school, where she lived and what music she liked. After a while Julie broke off the conversation and drifted back into the hall.

For the rest of the evening I spent most of my time outside the building, meeting and conversing with young people, reevaluating my earlier conclusion that this live band concept was a really bad idea. I got to know—at least by first name—many of the young people who had come to the event. Most were there because of a personal invitation and relationship with a member of the youth group. Few had turned up just because they had seen the flyer we had produced and distributed at the local high school. The success or otherwise of this outreach venture was clearly dependent on our capacity to build upon existing relationships.

Around midnight most of the young people had left and we started packing up. By the time we had finished packing the equipment in the van and cars it was the early hours of the morning. I was just about to leave when I noticed Julie sitting on the curb near the entrance of the hall. I walked over and offered to give her a ride home. Her reply was, "I can't go home." As I sat beside her on the curb she explained to me that she lived with her father and her father got drunk on the weekends and often beat her up. He had physically thrown her out of the house a number of times and told her he didn't want her living with him anymore. Julie had lost all contact with her mother. Her father had been drinking that night and she had come to our event because she really didn't have anywhere else to go. Her plan was to hang out on the streets until morning and then try to find a friend who would let her crash at their place for the day.

So here I was confronted with a dilemma. It was late, I was exhausted, and to be honest, I just wanted to go home and not have to deal with a teenage girl in a difficult situation. The Live Band Coffee Shop ministry plan was that young people would come to the program, get connected to young people in the church, come to Jesus and become part of the local church community. The event was meant to start at 7 p.m. and finish at midnight, at which time the young people would all go home and I would go home. It was not supposed to invade my personal space or time.

As I sat on the curb with Julie I was desperately trying to come up with a solution for her that didn't involve me. It was at that moment of indecision and inaction that the words I had recently read in James jumped into my head:

> Suppose a brother or sister is without clothes
> and daily food. If one of you says to him, "Go,
> I wish you well; keep warm and well fed," but
> does nothing about his physical needs, what
> good is it? In the same way, faith by itself, if it is
> not accompanied by action, is dead.[2]

The conviction of the Holy Spirit to do something for this girl was undeniable. But surely the Lord didn't expect me to take her home with me. We had a very small house and no room to accommodate her. What would my wife Jenny think if I turned up with a teenage girl in the middle of the night? I only had one day off a week, and if I took Julie home my day off would be spent trying to deal with her problems.

But no excuse was sufficient in the context of the clear direction I was getting from God. Did I have a living faith or a dead faith? I knew what I had to do. I asked Julie if she would like to stay at our home that night. I told her I would help her find a long-term solution to her living situation, and that she could stay with us until we did. As I offered these things to Julie, I could see the look of relief in her eyes. She was very close to tears. I took her home. Jenny found a mattress and made up a bed on the floor of our living room. Julie stayed with us until we found more permanent accommodation.

I kept in contact with Julie and after a while she started attending our church youth programs. Eventually Julie gave her life to Jesus and became an active member of the church. She started reaching out to her friends and a number of them also became believers.

Kingdom Impact

When Jesus was asked by his disciples how they should pray, he provided them with a model of prayer that has become known by his followers throughout history as "The Lord's Prayer."[3]

> Our Father in heaven,
> hallowed be your name,
> your kingdom come,
> your will be done
> on earth as it is in heaven.
> Give us today our daily bread.

Forgive us our debts,

as we also have forgiven our debtors.

And lead us not into temptation,

but deliver us from the evil one.

In this simple but profound prayer Jesus provides guidelines for our petitions and requests to God, but it is far more than a catalogue of subjects we should address in prayer; it is a list of imperatives for those who follow Jesus. After acknowledging and worshipping our Father in heaven, the first thing Jesus instructs us to ask for in our prayers is that God's Kingdom come and his will be done on earth as it is in heaven. Jesus tells us in Matthew 6:33 to "seek first his kingdom and his righteousness." Establishing God's Kingdom and working to see his will done on earth is an essential part of following and serving Jesus.

In 2 Corinthians 5:20 we are told we are "Christ's ambassadors." An ambassador is an authorized messenger or representative sent by a sovereign or state to speak and act on behalf of the sending authority. As followers of Jesus we are emissaries of the Kingdom of God, commissioned with the task of representing Jesus and establishing and advancing his rule on earth.

How does belonging to the Kingdom of God make a difference to the people around you? We all have a "circle of influence," people we encounter on a daily or weekly basis— relatives and friends, acquaintances, fellow students, work colleagues. How does our relationship with Jesus impact their lives? In Luke 17:21 Jesus states "the kingdom of God is within you." If we are authentic followers of Jesus the Kingdom of God should infuse our lives, and when people encounter us they should encounter the Kingdom.

Despite my reluctance, through the grace of God and the prompting of the Holy Spirit, a needy and essentially homeless girl encountered the Kingdom of God, and it radically changed her life. The little seed of the Kingdom that I sowed in Julie's life grew and blossomed, producing redemptive fruit that resulted in many others being touched by the Kingdom. The power of the Kingdom of God to change lives is inestimable, and we have free access to this unlimited transformational power. However, we also have the power of choice, and we can choose whether we release this Kingdom power, or withhold it.

When John the Baptist announced the coming of Jesus he said "Repent, for the kingdom of heaven is near."[4] As the Son of God, Jesus came to this earth to establish his father's Kingdom. In seeking to understand what it means for the Kingdom of God to come in our life and in the world, we need to look closely at the life of Jesus. Jesus was the purveyor of the Kingdom. As we explore what happened when Jesus interacted with humankind in his time on earth, the values, priorities and characteristics of the Kingdom will become abundantly clear.

In 1 John 2:6 we are told, "Whoever claims to live in him must walk as Jesus did." If we are followers of Jesus the life of Jesus should define who we are and what we do in this world. Studying the life of Jesus and identifying the principles and practices of the Kingdom are essential steps for us to express the Kingdom in our daily interaction with the world. But discovery is only the first step; discovery without application has no value in the Kingdom. "Walking as Jesus did" implies action. If we claim to be followers of Jesus, our lives should mirror the life of our Lord and Savior in practical ways. "Belief in" Jesus does not necessarily equate to "following" Jesus.

James 2:17 states, "Faith by itself, if it is not accompanied by action, is dead." Authentic followers of Jesus should impact, challenge and change the world as did Jesus when he walked this earth. Things that were evident when Jesus interacted with humanity two thousand years ago should also be evident when followers of Jesus interact with humanity today. That is why it is so important to not only identify the principles and practices of the Kingdom, but to live by them in the context of our daily interactions with the world around us.

When people asked Jesus what was required to be a part of the Kingdom he responded with two challenges: "Give up everything else in your life" and "Follow me." To the rich young ruler Jesus said, "Sell everything you have and give to the poor, and you will have treasure in heaven. Then come, follow me."[5] When he invited his disciples to join him he simply said, "Come, follow me," and they immediately gave up everything—career, possessions, family, home, reputation— and followed him.[6] Speaking to Jesus on behalf of the disciples Peter said, "We have left everything to follow you!"[7]

Following Jesus should radically impact your life. When Paul was confronted with Jesus on the Damascus road it completely turned his life upside-down. He went from persecuting followers of Jesus to being a radical disciple of

Jesus, giving up everything of his past life for the sake of the Kingdom.

Throughout the New Testament account of the early Church, followers of Jesus stood out among the general population because of their radical lifestyle. They were characterized by courageous representation of Jesus, self-denial, unprecedented generosity, unconditional love for others, simplicity of faith and commitment to community.

As followers of Jesus—people of the Kingdom—we should stand out among the crowd of humanity around us. We should be radically different—in a positive way—attracting people to the Kingdom by living in a way that epitomizes Jesus. We should be known for our self-sacrifice, love, generosity, loose attachment to things of this world, humility, gentleness, grace and courageous stand for justice and truth.

In this book we will explore what happens—or what should happen—when the Kingdom of God truly comes in us, in the church, in our local community and in the world. We will look at the things that should be evident when God's Kingdom intersects with the world, identify the challenges and opportunities associated with Kingdom living, and define practical responses to what we discover about the Kingdom and God's will.

May his Kingdom come, may his will be done in my life and yours, in the Church and in the world around us.

CHAPTER 1

When the Kingdom Comes . . .

PEOPLE WILL KNOW JESUS

Whoever claims to live in him must walk as Jesus did.
(1 John 2:6)

Paul had finally arrived in India. After developing a very successful medical practice in Australia, Paul and his wife Rebecca had become more and more convinced that God was calling them to "take Jesus" to the lost and needy people of India. Obediently pursuing their call, Paul and Rebecca sold their medical practice, rented out their house, sold or gave away most of their possessions, packed up their family and made the move.

The first year in India was not easy. Paul and Rebecca faced many emotionally draining challenges: adjusting to the local culture and living conditions, settling their children into school, establishing new friendships, practicing medicine with antiquated medical equipment and limited testing facilities, and connecting with indigenous and expatriate staff at the hospital. But, by far the hardest thing to cope with was the response of the patients at the hospital to Paul's efforts to tell them about Jesus.

Being a "missionary doctor," Paul had determined that he needed to tell everyone he came in contact with about

Jesus and their need to be "saved." He didn't want anyone to miss out on knowing the Jesus he loved and served. But as he shared the message of salvation with each patient, his efforts were either met with a wall of silence, rejection or—even more disturbing—a willingness to immediately accept Jesus as another god to be added to the pantheon of gods already worshiped in the context of the Hindu religion.

To those who would listen, Paul did his best to explain that Jesus was the only way, the only truth and the only source of eternal life; that to follow Jesus you needed to relinquish all other gods and serve and worship him alone. However, after a year of evangelical fervor, Paul had to admit that he had seen no genuine conversions to Christianity. He was bitterly disappointed and started to question his calling to ministry. He had developed a genuine and deep compassion for the people he was serving, which made him even more despondent that he was unable to convince them of their need for Jesus. Paul decided that he would no longer "tell" these people about Jesus, but simply provide medical services to them and do his best to alleviate their physical suffering. He and Rebecca started making plans to move back to Australia.

One day, while Paul was treating one of his long-term patients, the man asked him why he had given up his lucrative and comfortable life in Australia to come and live in such a poor area of the world to care for people no one else cared about. Without thinking Paul simply shared about his relationship with Jesus and his desire to serve Jesus by serving others. The man continued to question Paul about this "Jesus" he kept referring to, and Paul continued to answer his questions explaining what he believed about the identity of Jesus and what it was like to have a relationship with him. After chatting for several hours, the man finally stated, "I don't know this Jesus you are talking about, but if he is anything like you, I want to get to know him."

This man eventually gave his life to Jesus, and as the people of his community saw and experienced the transformational power of the Kingdom in his life, they too wanted to know this Jesus that he now represented.

Paul and Rebecca continued for many more years in their ministry in India, simply "living" Jesus rather than "telling about" Jesus. Many others came to faith and were discipled within the context of an active and authentic community of indigenous followers of Jesus.[8]

Telling Versus Living

When Jesus walked this earth he connected with people relationally. He met with them, conversed with them, taught them, debated with them, loved them, cared for them— shared his life with them. They knew him personally. When people meet representatives of Jesus, they should not simply "know about" Jesus, they should "know" Jesus. Wherever the Kingdom comes in this world people should meet Jesus.

Unfortunately, much of the "evangelical" activity of the church is predicated on a paradigm of "telling people about Jesus" rather than "living Jesus" in the context of interpersonal relationship. We are told we need to witness to others, to make a good defense for the faith, to campaign for Christ, to stand up and be counted.

Paul and Rebecca commenced their ministry in India with a model of evangelism that compelled them to "make a case" for Jesus. The problem with this approach is that it ends up being more about us and our worldview than about the person of Jesus. It is an "adversarial approach" that compels us to present our faith and understanding of the world as superior to the belief system of those we are trying to reach. The focus is on us and what we believe, and the image of Jesus is often blurred by our ardent advocacy.

Journalist Max Harris captured well the way many followers of Jesus are received when they take this adversarial approach. He observed: "Christians are a dim, ego-tripping minority which is dead set on telling everybody why they ought to become Christians, instead of finding out why they're not." Harris was reacting to what he perceived to be the arrogance of Christians, which is ironic considering how strongly we are compelled in Philippians to model the humility of Jesus.

> Do nothing out of selfish ambition or vain conceit, but in humility consider others better than yourselves. Each of you should look not only to your own interests, but also to the interests of others.

> Your attitude should be the same as that of Christ Jesus: Who, being in very nature God, did not consider equality with God something to be grasped, but made himself nothing, taking the very nature of a servant, being made in human likeness. And being found in appearance as a man, he humbled himself and became obedient to death—even death on a cross![9]

Tragically, it would appear that at the time Max Harris wrote this acerbic comment he hadn't met Jesus in any of the encounters he had with Christians. Instead of being won over by the humility of Jesus, Harris was repelled by the superior and conceited attitude of those who claimed to be his followers. Rather than conveying the person of Jesus, it appears that the Christians Harris had met had supplanted the spirit of Jesus in their life with their own "personalized" version of who he should be. Harris wasn't able to even get a glimpse of the real Jesus.

Fullness of Christ

The advancement of God's Kingdom is intrinsically tied to how much we allow Jesus to live in and through us, to how "full" we are of Jesus. This state of "fullness of Christ" is described in Ephesians:

> I pray that out of his glorious riches he may strengthen you with power through his Spirit in your inner being, so that Christ may dwell in your hearts through faith. And I pray that you, being rooted and established in love, may have power, together with all the saints, to grasp how wide and long and high and deep is the love of Christ, and to know this love that surpasses knowledge— that you may be filled to the measure of all the fullness of God. (Ephesians 3:16)

> And God placed all things under his feet and appointed him to be head over everything for the church, which is his body, the fullness

of him who fills everything in every way.
(Ephesians 1:22)

"Fullness" should be the ultimate objective of all followers of Jesus—both individually and collectively. But how do we achieve this fullness; this level of relationship with Jesus that enables us to authentically represent him to others? So much can get in the way: deeply ingrained personal and societal values; desires inconsistent with the values of the Kingdom that can be difficult to identify and even more difficult to overcome; misguided zeal—often driven by a genuine desire to share Jesus—that usually ends up with us forcing ourselves on others, devaluing their individual life journey and representing ourselves as the ones who have all the answers.

We are human beings, sinners saved by grace but still struggling with the sin that pulls us in all kinds of directions that are contrary to what and who Jesus wants us to be. Yet we have been given the commission and responsibility to share Jesus with the world. When people meet us, or when they encounter a community of believers, how clear is the image of Jesus? What does fullness in Christ really look like and how do we achieve this?

Behavior Modification

Even a genuine desire to authentically represent Jesus can drive us in all kinds of directions. Unfortunately, the starting point for many in their walk with Christ is to work hard at adhering to a prescribed code of behavior.

Repentance—turning from our old way of living to a new way of living—is a key tenet of the Christian faith. Working out what needs to change in our life, defining a set of behaviors consistent with the teachings of the Bible and then living by these new standards, would seem to be a logical approach to "being" a Christian.

But "behavior modification," rather than enhancing the quality of our relationship with Jesus, works against the spontaneity and sensitivity that is so intrinsic to healthy relationships. When we approach our relationship with Jesus behaviorally, the emphasis is more on our capacity to live up to a catalogue of self-imposed standards than it is about getting to know Jesus and allowing him to speak into and through our life.

The apostle Paul explains in detail how frustrating and inadequate this approach to living for Jesus can be:

> We know that the law is spiritual; but I am
> unspiritual, sold as a slave to sin. I do not
> understand what I do. For what I want to do
> I do not do, but what I hate I do. And if I do
> what I do not want to do, I agree that the law is
> good. As it is, it is no longer I myself who do it,
> but it is sin living in me.
>
> I know that nothing good lives in me, that is,
> in my sinful nature. For I have the desire to do
> what is good, but I cannot carry it out. For what
> I do is not the good I want to do; no, the evil I
> do not want to do—this I keep on doing.
>
> Now if I do what I do not want to do, it is no
> longer I who do it, but it is sin living in me that
> does it. So I find this law at work: When I want

to do good, evil is right there with me. For in
my inner being I delight in God's law; but I see
another law at work in the members of my body,
waging war against the law of my mind and
making me a prisoner of the law of sin at work
within my members.

What a wretched man I am! Who will rescue
me from this body of death?[10]

Behavior modification didn't work for Paul and I see no
reason why we would believe that it could or should work
for us. Yet, behavior modification seems to be the default
for many followers of Jesus and local church communities.
Driven by a desire to live like Jesus, we set ourselves the task
of behaving in a way that we believe aligns with who Jesus
wants us to be. We identify things we should and shouldn't
do, and then we set out to live according to the behavioral
code we have defined. Often it starts off well, we diligently
apply the "new rules," we behave better than we did before; we
feel pretty good about the changes we have made. But it is not
long before our guard slips. Our discipline falters and we fail
one or more of the behavioral tests we have set ourselves. Yet,
perseverance is one of the virtues upheld in the Bible; so we
pick ourselves up and renew our efforts to comply with our
new set of behaviors, enthusiastically pursuing the pathway to
authenticity. But we slip up again and again. The failures stack
up and eventually we regress back into who we were before
we applied the new rules. Ultimately, we fail to live up to our
self-imposed expectations of Jesus-like behavior; we become
discouraged and often self-condemning.

Inevitably, the failure of behavioral modification drives many down one of two pathways—*complacency* or *legalism*—both of which can take us further from our objective to be more like Jesus.

Complacency

The pathway to complacency usually begins with an adjustment of our expectations to a more moderate and "doable" set of behaviors. But unfortunately, because the whole behavior modification system is fatally flawed, any version of it is going to ultimately fail. When our new "lower" standard doesn't work, we are once again faced with our inability to live up to our self-imposed, though modified, standards. Permanent change seems to be an elusive goal, unattainable by sheer willpower and self-discipline. To compound our sense of inadequacy, as we analyze our serial failure we realize that even during the times when we actually managed to comply with our behavioral code, it didn't seem to result in us being more effective at characterizing Jesus.

Eventually, we give up. We settle for mediocrity. Our complacency defines who we are and we tend to just go through the motions of "being a Christian," having little or no impact on those around us. The people in our circle of influence may know that we go to church, that we are "Christians," but they never really get to meet or know Jesus. Far from being radical followers of Jesus, we are largely indistinguishable from the general population outside the Kingdom, exhibiting the same values, lifestyle, passions and inhibitions. The only difference is that we have the label "Christian."

The Bible describes this state of complacency as being

"lukewarm," and God says that when he encounters someone like this it makes him want to "vomit."[11] His desire is that people be either "hot or cold."[12] Instead of going through the motions of being a Christian and misrepresenting him, God would rather we not even identify ourselves as followers of Jesus.

When we become followers of Jesus we hand our life over to him—we give him total control. A relationship with Jesus is an "all or nothing" relationship. Jesus won't have it any other way! In Matthew 16:24 Jesus says, "If anyone would come after me, he must deny himself and take up his cross and follow me. For whoever wants to save his life will lose it, but whoever loses his life for me will find it."

Jesus died for us and he asks us to die for him. For new life to occur—to be "born again"—we need to die to our self. If we won't totally give up the control of our life, Jesus can't live through us. By engaging in behavioral modification we are still trying to control our life, and Jesus will not be free to recreate us in his image.

Legalism

The second pathway people may be driven down, after failing to live up to their own behavioral expectations, is one of a more rigorous application of rules and regulations. It is the pathway of "legalism," the very thing that Jesus went out of his way to condemn in his encounters with the religious leaders of his time.[13] These legalists were so afraid of breaking God's law that they built strict codes of behavior based on their interpretation of revealed law in the Pentateuch (the first five books of the Bible) and applied them rigorously to themselves and to those in their religious communities.

Legalism is generally defined as "a strict conformity to the letter of the law rather than its spirit."[14] This describes well the problem Jesus had with the Pharisees and teachers of the law:

> Woe to you, teachers of the law and Pharisees, you hypocrites! You give a tenth of your spices—mint, dill and cummin. But you have neglected the more important matters of the law—justice, mercy and faithfulness. You should have practiced the latter, without neglecting the former.[15]

It is generally in the context of a well-organized religious or political community that legalism thrives. It is rare to find an individualized legalism that begins and ends with one person. Legalism needs community to work; it requires controlling leaders who define and enforce behavioral codes, and a compliant community of followers who conform to and reinforce the control of the leadership through monitoring and reporting mechanisms.

The systematized rule-driven form of faith espoused by the Pharisees was an anathema to Jesus. It replaced a personal relationship with God with a performance-based religious system that was unrelentingly administered by self-appointed arbitrators who assumed a role of absolute power and control. Jesus said of these religious leaders and their legalistic systems of control:

> Woe to you, teachers of the law and Pharisees, you hypocrites! You shut the kingdom of heaven

in men's faces. You yourselves do not enter, nor
will you let those enter who are trying to.

Woe to you, teachers of the law and Pharisees,
you hypocrites! You travel over land and sea to
win a single convert, and when he becomes one,
you make him twice as much a son of hell as you
are.[16]

Once, having been asked by the Pharisees when
the kingdom of God would come, Jesus replied,
"The kingdom of God does not come with your
careful observation."[17]

So why would people who seek to follow Jesus and
advance his Kingdom gravitate to faith communities that
employ religious systems that Jesus himself identified as
unacceptable? I believe it is because these communities offer
a clearly defined way for people to achieve a standard they
perceive as necessary for them to be acceptable to God. They
realize they can't achieve this standard on their own—and
they struggle to even work out the non-negotiable behaviors
and compliances of "being a Christian"—so they join with
others who can define for them what is required to be "right
with God."

In a legalistic religious system, formulas are applied to
all aspects of life and faith. There is a sense of security in
knowing that by adhering to a particular set of behaviors you
are "in." It also makes it easy to define who is "out," and to
communicate to those who are "out" what they need to do
to get "in." In contrast to trying to live up to a self-imposed

behavioral code—which we have seen almost always ends in failure and frustration—community-imposed legalism is far easier to comply with. Living as a "Christian" by having others tell you how to live, as well as keeping you accountable to the prescribed standards of behavior, is eminently possible. However, Jesus doesn't leave the legalism option open to us, for he rejects and condemns adherence to a set of rules as the way of faith and service in his Kingdom.

In Romans Paul goes to great lengths to explain how we are no longer under law but under grace.[18] In Corinthians and Galatians he contrasts a life of legalism with the Spirit-led life, stating that strict adherence to a set of laws "kills," whereas the Spirit gives life.[19] Cluttering our life with rules, regulations and behavioral compliances leaves little room for Jesus. If we are in control, then God isn't, and Jesus is not free to fully operate in and through us.

Grace

Aside from being condemned by Jesus, legalism has no place in God's Kingdom because it kills grace. The grace that is offered to us through Jesus is the very distinctive of the Kingdom that sets it apart from all other faiths and religions. In his book *What's So Amazing About Grace*, Philip Yancey relates a story about C. S. Lewis that highlights the uniqueness of grace:

> During a British conference on comparative
> religions, experts from around the world
> debated what, if any, belief was unique to
> the Christian faith. They began eliminating
> possibilities. Incarnation? Other religions had

different versions of gods appearing in human
form. Resurrection? Again, other religions
had accounts of return from death. The debate
went on for some time until C. S. Lewis
wandered into the room. "What's all the rumpus
about?" he asked, and heard in reply that his
colleagues were discussing Christianity's unique
contribution among world religions. Lewis
responded, "Oh, that's easy. It's grace."

After some discussion, the conferees had to
agree. The notion of God's love coming to us
free of charge, no strings attached, seems to go
against every instinct of humanity. The Buddhist
eight-fold path, the Hindu doctrine of *karma*,
the Jewish covenant, and Muslim code of law—
each of these offers a way to earn approval.
Only Christianity dares to make God's love
unconditional.[20]

Grace is "unmerited favor to the ill-deserving." The theme
runs through the whole Bible. It is founded on the premise
that there is nothing we can do to put things right with God
or to live up to the standard that God requires for citizenship
in his Kingdom. Only by an act of grace can things be made
right between us and God.

But now a righteousness from God, apart from
law, has been made known, to which the Law
and the Prophets testify. This righteousness
from God comes through faith in Jesus Christ
to all who believe. There is no difference, for all

have sinned and fall short of the glory of God,
and are justified freely by his grace through the
redemption that came by Christ Jesus.

For we maintain that a man is justified by faith
apart from observing the law.[21]

When we understand grace it becomes abundantly clear
why following a set of laws or behaviors will not enable us to
become more like Jesus or enhance our capacity to advance
his Kingdom. Citizenship in the Kingdom is solely based
upon our relationship with Jesus, and therefore Jesus must be
the touch-point for those we are endeavoring to invite into
the Kingdom. Presenting a set of cultural norms or a codex of
prescribed behaviors as the means by which someone enters
the Kingdom of God doesn't align with the foundations of
the Christian faith—grace, faith and unconditional love.

Intimacy with Jesus

Allowing Jesus to live through us is the only way for us to
accurately represent the Kingdom. When those outside the
Kingdom encounter people of the Kingdom they should meet
Jesus, they should experience his unconditional acceptance,
they should be overwhelmed by his grace, and they should be
captivated by his love.

By simply loving and caring for those they were called to
reach in India, Paul and Rebecca allowed Jesus to live through
them. The people who encountered Paul in the hospital
were no longer confronted with someone who was trying
to convince them of the fallacy of their worldview. Instead
they experienced Jesus in person and were drawn to his love,

compassion, acceptance and humility. They encountered Jesus in their relationship with Paul.

So how do we achieve the "fullness in Christ" that is described in Ephesians 4? What is the secret to having Jesus so fill us that he controls our relational interactions, our emotional responses, our values and our very character? The biblical imperative to "walk as Jesus did"[22] is obviously a huge challenge to all who would follow Jesus. If the legalistic approach doesn't work, then what does? Surely there has to be some form of dedication to a systematic way of living that will allow Jesus to take control and shine through our life?

In the end it is not rules or systems that determine our capacity to convey Jesus to others; it is the quality of our relationship with Jesus—our closeness to him. It is all about intimacy with Christ. The old saying "more of him and less of me" is the key to effectively sharing Jesus with the world.

If we are people of the Kingdom, Jesus should define who we are. This is what Paul was driving at when he said in Philippians 2:13, "For it is God who works in you to will and to act according to his good purpose." Immersing ourselves in Jesus is the key to representing him authentically.

This level of closeness to Jesus can only be achieved by making our relationship with Jesus an absolute priority. We need to be disciplined in our prayer life, spending exclusive and substantial time with Jesus, talking things over with him and listening to his voice. We need to make spending time with Jesus more important than doing things for Jesus. We need to be immersed in his Word, studying the life of Jesus and applying the truth of the Bible to our life. And we need to be accountable for the time we spend with Jesus, making deliberate changes and setting up accountability structures that ensure that we have "exclusive" time with Jesus every day.

As we spend more and more time with Jesus he will identify the areas that we are holding back from him, and he will take over more and more of our life. The secret to living as Jesus would is to live in a state of constant awareness of Jesus' presence. Only then will we be able to instinctively respond as Jesus would to every situation.

Spiritual Formation

The state of our heart

The Bible consistently talks about spiritual fruit and the character of Christ coming from a changed heart. For instance, "The good man brings good things out of the good stored up in his heart, and the evil man brings evil things out of the evil stored up in his heart. For out of the overflow of his heart his mouth speaks."[23] In 1 Timothy 1:5 Paul states that love "comes from a pure heart and a good conscience and a sincere faith." The heart is the inner core of a person's being, and unless the heart is transformed, it will be enormously difficult to respond to life situations with the values and character of Christ. The fruit of the Spirit and the grace of God will flow naturally from a heart that has been transformed by God, yet it is only through the transformational work of the Holy Spirit that the heart can be changed. If we are to love others with the love of Jesus, then we have to pay attention to our heart.

In 1 Samuel 16:7 we are told, "The Lord does not look at the things man looks at. Man looks at the outward appearance, but the Lord looks at the heart." The main problem with behavior modification and legalism is that they focus upon *what* we should do or not do, rather than *who* we are. As we have seen in his interaction with the Pharisees and teachers of the law, Jesus is much more concerned about character—about the intrinsic values that drive our life—than he is about observation of a catalogue of "do's" and "don'ts."

In Matthew Jesus tells us that it is by our "fruit" that others will know whether or not we are followers of him.[24] In Galatians we are given a list of spiritual fruit: "love, joy, peace, patience, kindness, goodness, faithfulness, gentleness and self-control."[25] Our spiritual fruitfulness is the ultimate test of our authenticity.

The only way we are going to be able to exhibit this fruit in our life is to live by the Spirit. It is not going to come naturally, nor are we going to be able to force these attributes into our life. In Ephesians 5:18 we read, "Do not get drunk on wine, which leads to debauchery. Instead, be filled with the Spirit." When you are drunk you lose control of yourself and the effect of the alcohol takes over. Paul likens being filled with the Spirit to being drunk. We need to be "drunk" on the Spirit, to be filled to such a degree that it is not us directing our actions and thoughts but the Spirit. The more we open ourselves up to Jesus by spending time with him, the more we allow his Spirit to fill us, and the more we will be like him.

The Spiritual Formation movement

Over the past decade increasing attention has been given to the subject of "spiritual formation." Books have been written, spiritual formation conferences organized, Bible studies developed and processes implemented—all directed at encouraging and enabling people in the Church to better represent Jesus by who they are and how they live. This movement has been driven by a deepening concern that the religious structures and institutions of Christianity are no longer producing authentic followers of Jesus, but are rather churning out a population of shallow, self-serving, judgmental, culturally superior individuals who are misrepresenting Jesus and his Church to a watching world. It is a rejection of the "religiosity" of Christianity and the accompanying loss of intimacy with Jesus that is driving people to pursue a new experience of Jesus and his transformational power in their lives.

We can learn much from the spiritual formation movement and I would encourage you to investigate further its concepts and precepts. However, the point I want to make about this movement is that this quest for a new intimacy with God has identified the "transformation of the heart" as the key element in the spiritual formation of a person into the image of Jesus.

Dallas Willard, one of the leading lights in the spiritual formation movement, states:

> Spiritual formation in the tradition of Jesus
> Christ is the process of transformation of the
> inmost dimension of the human being, the
> heart, which is the same as the spirit or will. It is
> being formed (really, transformed) in such a way
> that its natural expression comes to be the deeds
> of Christ done in the power of Christ.[26]

Willard goes on to point out that there is both "a passive element and an active element" to spiritual formation. He observes:

We know, as Jesus says, "Without me you can do nothing." (John 15:5) . . . It is the initiative of God and the presence of God without which all of our efforts are in vain—whether it is in justification or sanctification or in the realm of the exercise of power, all our efforts will be in vain if God does not act. But we had better believe that the back side of that verse reads: "If you do nothing it will be without me." And this is the part we have the hardest time hearing.

Referring to Proverbs 23:19 Willard says:

"Keep your heart." Well, that's something for me to do. I have the keeping of my heart. I am responsible for it. Do I do it alone? No. If I do it alone, I'll just make bad matters worse. But I have to do it nonetheless. I am the one who has to "give all diligence to add to my faith moral excellence and add to my moral excellence knowledge"—I'm the one. Again: Do I do it alone? No. But if I do nothing, it will not be done.

Willard is pointing out that it is God who transforms the heart, but that we need to allow him to transform it and be involved in the transformational process.

The spiritual formation movement is characterized by a number of disciplines: contemplative prayer, life-impacting worship, immersion in God's Word, self-denial and sacrificial service. This is not pseudo behaviorism; it is the application of God's truth through discipline and diligence. It is not forcing behavioral change, but it is dedication to a set of practices and activities that provide opportunity for greater intimacy with Jesus and deep heart renovation by the Holy Spirit. It requires us to do something to place ourselves in a position where God can transform us.

Paul talks about spiritually forming discipline in 1 Corinthians 9:24–27:

> Do you not know that in a race all the runners run, but only one gets the prize? Run in such a way as to get the prize. Everyone who competes in the games goes into strict training. They do it to get a crown that will not last; but we do it to get a crown that will last forever.
>
> Therefore I do not run like a man running aimlessly; I do not fight like a man beating the air. No, I beat my body and make it my slave so that after I have preached to others, I myself will not be disqualified for the prize.

Spiritual disciplines and activities that place us in an environment where the Holy Spirit can work on our hearts and renew our minds[27] are the key to us developing our capacity to characterize Jesus.

Pray Continually[28]

In 1 Thessalonians 5:17 we are instructed to "pray continually." What does Paul mean by this? Obviously he did more than pray all day. Yet what he conveys in this directive seems to suggest that we should be constantly in prayer.

The *Zondervan NIV Bible Commentary* provides a helpful

explanation of this verse. "'Continually' does not mean nonstop praying. Rather, it implies constantly recurring prayer, growing out of a settled attitude of dependence on God. Whether words are uttered or not, lifting the heart to God while one is occupied with miscellaneous duties is the vital thing. Verbalized prayer will be spontaneous and will punctuate one's daily schedule, as it did Paul's writings."[29]

The *Asbury Bible Commentary* provides further insight, "Prayer is the constant attitude of the believer. To 'pray continually' means that every activity must be carried on with a sense of God's presence."[30]

What this verse is about is intimacy with Jesus, living in an attitude of prayer that provides a continuous connection with our God and Saviour. Constantly spending time with Jesus deepens our relationship with him and allows intimacy to develop.

Listening to Jesus

When I was starting out in my ministry with Youth for Christ I was concerned that I was not spending enough time in prayer. I wanted to get closer to Jesus and to develop a deeper understanding of his plan for my life. At the same time I realized I needed to improve my fitness. So I decided to start walking for an hour every morning.

Trying to fit in a prayer time as well as an hour walk in the morning was a real struggle, and I just didn't seem to have enough time for both. Then it dawned on me, why couldn't I pray while I was walking? So that's what I did. I would spend an hour in the morning praying and walking. I also had a daily Bible reading schedule, so often I had verses that I was mulling over in my head as I walked.

The first few weeks of this regime, I would spend my whole walking hour talking to Jesus about issues, problems, needs and ministry plans. However, one morning I got a very strong sense from Jesus to just "shut up and listen." And so that's what I did. I started my walk by saying, "Okay Lord, I'm listening, please speak to me." I just walked and waited, and Jesus started to direct my thoughts to him and his character. I thought about his provision in my life and his grace and patience, and about his faithfulness and blessing, and as I walked and meditated on Jesus I was suddenly overwhelmed by a sense of his presence and love for me. At this moment Jesus directed my thoughts to a big problem I was having at Youth for Christ, and it was as if a light had been turned on. Jesus interwove his wisdom with my problem and provided an amazingly simple but brilliant solution that honored him and reflected his character. Up until this time I had been so busy telling Jesus about my problems that he couldn't get a word in. He just wanted me to listen. And when I did, he was able to provide the answer in the context of his character and faithfulness.

As I spent more time with Jesus, studying and meditating on his Word, and listening to him, I started to sense his presence with me throughout the day. I often found myself chatting to him about things as I encountered them in my ministry and family life. In my conversations with others I would sometimes say something and realize that what I said was not consistent with how I would have normally responded, but it was a far better response that resulted in a far better outcome. The closer we get to Jesus, the more he can live through us, directing our every thought, word and action.

Quality means quantity

Authentic Christian faith is expressed in our relationships—our relationship with Jesus, our relationship with fellow Christians, our relationship with our spouse and children, our relationship with others outside of God's family—and it is how we conduct these relationships that determines our capacity to represent Jesus and to live like him.

I am sure that you have heard the term "quality time." Spending quality time with our spouse or children is often presented as a relational panacea, as the "cure-all" for healthy relationships. But from my experience, the quality of the time we spend with family members is directly related to the quantity of time we spend with them. Availability is also a key factor in family relationships, because the amount of time we are prepared to devote to being available in a relationship conveys the priority we place upon that relationship.

Let me explain by using the example of the modern family. People's lives today are replete with activities and commitments. In fact, if you ask people how they are doing in life, they will often answer with one word—"busy." By the time children are in their teenage years, the parents, particularly fathers, are usually so busy in their careers and other activities that they have very little time available for their children.

In the context of this time-gobbling lifestyle, parents often grab hold of the notion that spending quality time with their children will make up for the little time they are available in the home. So they plan an activity to do with their teenage son or daughter that they believe will provide some "bonding" time with their child.

Let's say a father allocates some time in his busy schedule

to go to a movie with his teenage son, thinking this will enable them to have some quality time together. Unfortunately, the most likely response will be a dismissive rejection of the whole idea; and the reason given will probably be that his son already has other plans—or will be making plans—to do something with his friends.

The fact that the father has planned some "cool" activity with his son means very little to his child, because the activity is not offered in the context of a meaningful relationship with his father. What the son is looking for is a relationship where he knows he is a priority, where he matters to his father more than work or friends or other commitments. He is looking for a father who will be available when he needs him, who won't just brush him off saying he is too busy when the son needs help with a problem, or a ride to his friend's house, or a chat about something that happened at school. The quality of the relationship is directly proportional to the quantity of time the father is available and willing to spend with his son. Quality equals quantity and availability.

The same principles that apply to our relationships with other human beings apply to our relationship with Jesus. The quality of relationship with Jesus depends upon the quantity of time we spend with him. We need to be spending as much time as possible with Jesus, striving to be as close to him as we can so that he will be reflected in our lives. Busyness doesn't only prevent us from having healthy relationships with our family and friends; it also prevents us from having an intimate and life-changing relationship with Jesus. Prioritizing our life around Jesus is the key to being a true representation of him to the world.

You can't allocate times and dates in your calendar to accommodate a crisis with your son or daughter, or schedule the times that your children will need your advice because they are facing a major challenge. It simply won't work for you to say to your daughter, "Honey, I have an opening on Thursday evening between dinner and my leadership meeting at the church. Can we schedule for you to have a crisis in your relationship with your friend between 7 and 7:30 p.m. on Thursday?" Crises in your family generally come at the most inconvenient times. If you are going to faithfully serve your family, then your spouse and children need to have a place of priority in your life and take precedence over the other items in your weekly schedule.

In the same way, if you are going to faithfully represent and serve Jesus, spending time with him must take priority in your life. You can't just allocate a free slot in your schedule for Jesus and expect that this is going to provide all the relational connection you need to reach a level of spiritual maturity where people will see only Jesus and not you. Jesus is not going to be able to do much in your life if you tell him, "Well, this week I have an opening on Saturday at 7:30 a.m. when I can spend ten minutes with you." Our relationship with Jesus should be pervasive; it should permeate all areas of our life, not just a five- or ten-minute slot every so often.

Worshipping Daily

What is worship? We are told in Romans, "Offer your bodies as living sacrifices, holy and pleasing to God—this is your spiritual act of worship. Do not conform any longer to the pattern of this world, but be transformed by the renewing of your mind. Then you will be able to test and approve what God's will is—his good, pleasing and perfect will."[31]

In Micah we are given similar instructions:

With what shall I come before the LORD
and bow down before the exalted God?

Shall I come before him with burnt offerings,
with calves a year old?

Will the LORD be pleased with thousands of rams,
with ten thousand rivers of oil?
Shall I offer my firstborn for my transgression,
the fruit of my body for the sin of my soul?

He has showed you, O man, what is good.
And what does the LORD require of you?

To act justly and to love mercy
and to walk humbly with your God.[32]

Worshipping God as he requires is far more than meeting for a short time once a week to sing choruses and hymns; it is daily reflecting God in our lives and bringing glory to him through doing his will on this earth. It involves obedience and self-sacrifice. Worship is walking humbly through each day with Jesus in such a close and intimate relationship that it transforms and renews our thinking, allowing us to know the will of God and to bring him honor and glory daily by the way we live.

God's Word

Studying God's Word in and of itself will not result in transformation. Throughout history there have been many scholars of God's Word who have not exhibited the character of Christ or lived by the principles and values of the Scripture they were studying. The Pharisees and Teachers of the Law knew God's Word extensively, yet Jesus was quick to point out that they failed to let the Scripture change their lives.

In James 1:22–25 we are told:

> Do not merely listen to the word, and so deceive
> yourselves. Do what it says. Anyone who listens
> to the word but does not do what it says is
> like a man who looks at his face in a mirror
> and, after looking at himself, goes away and
> immediately forgets what he looks like. But the
> man who looks intently into the perfect law
> that gives freedom, and continues to do this, not
> forgetting what he has heard, but doing it—he
> will be blessed in what he does.

The study of God's Word must be seen as a spiritual activity, rather than a purely intellectual pursuit—the objective of our study is to meet Jesus and allow him to apply God's Word to our heart and mind. Jesus is identified in the Bible as the "Word of God";[33] he is the means by which God communicates his character and truth to us. Any encounter with the Bible should be an encounter with Jesus.

Reading God's Word with an open heart and mind, seeking the character of Christ and letting the Holy Spirit apply the Word to our life is a challenging proposition. It is so easy to slip into an analytical approach to God's Word, where we gather facts and information without seeing any real change in our life. Knowing the Bible is important, but knowing the author of the Bible is so much more important and is the key to transformation. Seeing the Bible as a means to deepen our relationship with Jesus will motivate us to look for Jesus in the words we are reading and studying. As we meet Jesus in the pages of the Bible our lives will be transformed.

Meditating on the Word

We should read the Bible expecting Jesus to speak to us. I have found that when I meditate on passages from the Bible my heart and mind are opened to Jesus and I have a greater sense of his direction and purpose for my life. Reflecting on what we read in the Bible—rather than simply reading a passage and moving on with the rest of our daily schedule—allows room for Jesus to apply the Word to our lives.

Journaling has helped me enormously in reflecting on the Word. This involves reading a passage of the Bible and then, in an attitude of prayer and listening, writing down what I think God is saying to me through the passage. Journaling helps me to get clarity and to work through the things that I have been confronted with in the Bible. On many occasions it has been transformational as I have gained a new understanding of Jesus and his purpose for my life.

I first started journaling when I attended a three-day prayer retreat with some other youth ministry leaders. I was actually reluctant to participate as I had never been on a prayer retreat before and I was wondering how I was going to cope with praying for three days. However, on the first day, the leaders of the retreat gave us a passage of Scripture and sent us off on our own to meditate on the passage and write down what we believed God was saying to us. We were given an hour to work through the text. As I read, meditated and wrote down my conversation with God, I was surprised at how quickly the hour went by. I was reluctant to return to the group as I had so much more I wanted to write and share with God. As the retreat progressed, we were given more and more time to read, meditate and journal. In just three days, my relationship with God grew to a new level of intimacy I had no idea was possible. As God applied his Word to my life, I became increasingly aware of my need for his forgiveness and healing. Things that I had ignored and hidden because they were too painful to deal with were exposed. God used his Word to minister to me, freeing me from guilt, bitterness and self-reliance. It was a life-changing experience.

Life application

God's Word should be the reference point for our lives. It should be the place we go to as we confront the challenges and opportunities that life constantly throws at us.

Often, early in our journey as believers we "hunger and thirst" for God's Word. We devour God's Word as we explore what it means to be a follower of Jesus, seeking answers in the Bible as we encounter the many questions and dilemmas that arise as we work out our new-found faith. But as we journey on in life, we get better at "being a Christian" and we don't "need" to refer as much to God's Word for the answers. We become "experts" and often end up dispensing the truth to others without direct reference to God's Word.

How we view and treat God's Word is often revealed in the way we interact with other believers. In my leadership role in Youth for Christ I have many opportunities to provide support and counsel to young people and Youth for Christ staff. Unfortunately, I am a "serial advice-giver." When I am asked about issues of life, ministry, relationships, values or calling I have a tendency to provide immediate answers drawing on my own experience and wisdom, telling those seeking my counsel what I think—what my experience has taught me—and applying it to their life situation.

If we believe the Bible is the ultimate authority for all we do, surely the best way for us to respond when asked for advice, counsel and guidance, is to go directly to God's Word. Instead of giving our answers and advice, a better response would be to say, "Let's go and see what God's Word says about that," and together explore and discover what the Bible says about the issue.

When we view the Bible as static information rather than the living Word of God, we tend not to return to it to regularly to seek answers to life's questions. We become "experts," thinking we know enough to speak with authority and to give advice to others less experienced and knowledgeable than us without going to God's Word and seeking the input and wisdom of God himself. However, if we treat the Bible as a living, vibrant and dynamic means for God to communicate with us, we will continually revisit the Word—even the passages we know well—expecting God to speak, to reveal something new about himself and about us.

Reading the Gospels

Over the years I have journeyed with Jesus I have encountered a number of people whom I highly respect as authentic followers of Jesus. When I have asked these people what they do to keep on track with Jesus, many of them have told me that they have a practice of reading through the Gospels[34] continuously. The rationale they provide for doing this is that it helps them to keep close to Jesus as they are confronted daily with an account of Jesus' life and teaching.

Studying and learning from the life and teachings of Jesus should be a lifetime pursuit of every one of his followers. Every time I read the Gospels I am amazed at how much I discover. Even though I have read these passages of the Bible many times before, as I read them again I gain new perspective, a deeper understanding of Jesus, and often a different application of the teachings of Jesus to my life.

There is great value in being a "serial consumer" of the Gospels.

Immersion in God's Word

One of the approaches I have found helpful in reading God's Word is to treat it more as a "story" than a "textbook" of facts and information. When you read large slabs of the Bible at one time you get a far greater sense of the truth and continuity of the message of God's Word and a more comprehensive picture of the character of God.

Recently I have started listening to the Bible. I purchased the Bible on CD and now play these CDs in my car as I drive to and from the office. This has helped me to appreciate the Bible as a whole, rather than a compilation of separate parts.

It has kept me from losing the overall context and wonder of this amazing God-inspired book.

Honesty & Truth

Immersion in God's Word keeps us honest. As James points out, reading the Word is like looking in a mirror[35] in that it reflects back to us our true nature.

Hebrews likens the Word to a sword. Hebrews 4:12–13 states:

> For the word of God is living and active.
> Sharper than any double-edged sword, it
> penetrates even to dividing soul and spirit,
> joints and marrow; it judges the thoughts and
> attitudes of the heart. Nothing in all creation
> is hidden from God's sight. Everything is
> uncovered and laid bare before the eyes of him
> to whom we must give account.

As we open ourselves up to the surgical knife of the Bible it exposes our true nature, cutting away the masks and protective lies we build around ourselves, revealing the hidden things in our life, reflecting back to us our true self.

Jesus described himself as "the way, the truth and the life."[36] His very nature is truth, and if we are to represent him accurately we need to be people of the truth. We need to be people who, in the truth-exposing light of God's Word, are honest about ourselves; people who find such security in the love and acceptance of Jesus that we can achieve a level of self-acceptance that allows us to be true and honest in the way we represent ourselves to others. We should be people who stand out because of our honesty—people who can be trusted to tell the truth and live by the truth.

Lies and deception are so much part of the fabric of our world that it is often hard to even recognize the truth, let alone live honest and truthful lives. Yet, although honesty is such a rare commodity, it seems people long for the truth; that there is such a voracious hunger for truth that when people encounter it they are captivated and crave more.

Dishonesty is one of the biggest impediments to us authentically communicating Jesus. If Jesus is "the truth" and we are not truthful, then how can we represent him to others?

Lying is a relational cancer, rapidly spreading tentacles of deceit that destroy trust and security—the vital elements of healthy relationships. One lie can lead to many other lies very quickly. For instance, let's say a guy named Sam is running late to work because he slept in. He knows his boss really gets annoyed when people turn up late to work without a good reason, so Sam calls his boss and tells him that he is going to be late because he has a flat tire on his car. When Sam gets to work the boss asks him where he was when he got the flat tire. Another lie is needed to back up Sam's first lie. Sam describes how he had to pull over on a busy road, adding details of the challenges of swapping the flat for the spare. The boss asks what caused the flat—once again Sam has to lie, telling his boss he found a screw in the tire. Sam's colleagues at work then ask him why he was late—more lies are needed to support the first lie. The web of deceit rapidly expands and Sam ends up having to lie many more times—and to many more people—than he originally intended to.

Fear is the driving force behind deception. You lie to

others because you fear the outcome of not lying. More lies are needed because of the fear of being discovered, and as the web of deception expands, so do the consequences of the lie. Simply telling the truth can be so freeing. If Sam had called his boss and told him he was going to be late for work because he overslept, the consequences would have most likely been a simple reprimand by his boss. But Sam would have been free from fear, free from the pressure to continue to lie to cover up his original deception, free to prove to his boss that he could do better.

Honesty is foundational to meaningful relationship. If we know that we can rely upon someone to tell the truth it creates an environment of security and trust. If people are truly honest in their interactions with each other, they no longer have to live with the tension of being exposed, of the other person finding out who they really are and rejecting them. They can relax and truly be themselves, not having to rely on lies to impress or buy acceptance or to cover up their perceived inadequacies.

In 1 John 4:18 we read that "perfect love drives out fear." The antithesis of love is fear; and fear is generated and reinforced by lies and deception.

In my relationship with Jenny, we try our best to be honest with each other. We have a security and deep trust in our marriage relationship that could not be possible if we were not committed to telling the truth. For example, if Jenny asks me if I like what she is wearing, she knows she will get an honest answer from me. I might not be very qualified to answer, because women's fashion is definitely not my strong suit. But Jenny knows I will tell her if I think the dress she is wearing doesn't look good on her. If I lied and said I thought it looked good when I didn't like it, why would she bother to ask me in the future? My opinion would have no value because Jenny could not trust me to give an honest answer. But Jenny—knowing that I love her and that the last thing I would want to do is to hurt her—can receive my answer, even if it is that I don't like the look of the dress. She is secure in the honesty and love of our marriage relationship.

The fact that Jenny can receive an honest opinion from me about the look of her clothing may seem like a simple issue, but if Jenny and I practice honesty in our day-to-day interactions—in the ordinary "stuff of life"—then this becomes the norm in our relationship. If honesty is intrinsic to our marriage relationship, then when the deeper issues of life arise, we are free to express the truth of what we are experiencing. Honesty provides the relational solidarity, acceptance and security we need to not only survive all that life throws at us, but to thrive in our life journey. We are free to be ourselves, knowing that we are accepted and loved for who we really are. True freedom comes by practicing the truth. Jesus declared in John 8:32, "The truth will set you free."

The biblical perspective

Jesus said that he came to give life and to give it to the full.[37] Truth is a key element to this fullness of life that Jesus desires for us. The Bible clearly states that lies and deception are an anathema to God and an impediment to all that God desires for us.

In Proverbs 12:22 we read, "The Lord detests lying lips, but he delights in men who are truthful." In Proverbs 6:16–17 we are told there are seven things the Lord hates; two of the seven are "a lying tongue" and "a false witness who pours out lies."

Jesus identifies the gravity of lying in John 8:44. When addressing a group of Jewish leaders he says: "You belong to your father, the devil, and you want to carry out your father's desire. He was a murderer from the beginning, not holding to the truth, for there is no truth in him. When he lies, he speaks his native language, for he is a liar and the father of lies."

Who are we representing when we deceive and lie? We are certainly not representing Jesus, and we are definitely not representing Kingdom values. The consequence of lying is that it disqualifies us from authentically representing Jesus and experiencing the fullness of life that he offers to all.

I have been greatly distressed over recent years as I have seen prominent Christian leaders discredited and failing because of serial lying and deception. The starting point of the demise of these leaders is generally associated with some form of moral indiscretion. Unfortunately, when challenged by a concerned spouse or fellow leaders who suspect something is amiss, they deny having a problem, usually fabricating a story to explain away the suspicion and concern. Without the accountability and loving intervention that comes with the truth, these flawed leaders continue down a pathway of self-perpetuating moral failure, ultimately requiring a web of lies so complex that it eventually collapses, exposing their duplicity and discrediting them and the one they claim to serve and follow.

Another disappointing phenomenon I am encountering of late is the perception that some Christian business leaders cannot be trusted. I have lost count of the number of times I have had someone say to me, "I am never going to do

business with a Christian again because they can't be trusted."
Dishonesty, insincerity, lack of integrity and deception
distort the image of Jesus to such a degree that he is virtually
unrecognizable.

Shining lights of integrity

As followers of Jesus we should be known as people of
impeccable integrity, as people of the truth. Throughout the
gospels Jesus tells us to be shining lights in the darkness. I
believe that one of the most effective ways to shine our light
in this world is to be honest, to be purveyors of the truth.

I have a friend who owns two car dealerships. Car
salespeople are often lampooned as the least trustworthy
people in society. My friend is a man of godly character who
loves Jesus and strives to live a life of integrity and truth. People
travel for miles to buy a vehicle from my friend's dealerships—
passing many other dealerships on the way—because they
know they will receive honest service. He is open about his
faith and he demands that his sales and administrative staff
adhere to the values of the Kingdom. People are drawn to
the light of Jesus expressed in the truth and integrity being
practiced by this follower of Jesus in a business sector known
for deception and lack of integrity.

When Jesus, the source of truth, reigns in us, his Kingdom
comes and honesty and integrity will prevail.

Following Jesus—being citizens of the Kingdom of
God—is more about who we are than what we do, because
what we do is determined by who we are. It is more about
character formation than behavior modification, because our

behaviors are derived from our character. It is more about compassion than obligation, because it is out of love for God that we are compelled to love others. And, it is more about relationship than it is about religion, because it is through a relationship with Jesus that we enter the Kingdom of God.

Jesus came to save us from ourselves. Following him involves dying to self so that we can be reborn into the Kingdom. In God's Kingdom, we are not citizens by immigration; we are citizens by rebirth. Jesus calls those who follow him "sons of the Kingdom"[38] and "sons of God."[39] In Galatians we are told "You are all sons of God through faith in Christ Jesus"[40] and that as heirs we have received the "the full rights of sons."[41] When we follow Jesus we not only become citizens of the Kingdom of God, we become sons and daughters of the King. However, to take our place in the Kingdom we need to forfeit our life; we need to give everything to Jesus—money, possessions, career, family and life itself—so that Jesus can recreate us in his image. Handing ourselves over to Jesus provides him with the freedom to use us to shine the light of his love and character into the world.

May we be able to say with Paul, "I have been crucified with Christ and I no longer live, but Christ lives in me."

We would see Jesus

In John 12 we read of some Greeks approaching one of Jesus' disciples and saying, "We would see Jesus."[42] Many in the world today are searching for the truth, longing to find the way to fullness of life, and are requesting of those who claim to be people of the Kingdom: "We would see Jesus."

May we be the instruments by which people see Jesus. May people meet Jesus when they meet us.

CHAPTER 2

When the Kingdom Comes . . .

THE GOOD NEWS WILL BE PROCLAIMED

But you will receive power when the Holy Spirit comes on you; and you will be my witnesses in Jerusalem, and in all Judea and Samaria, and to the ends of the earth.
(Acts 1:8)

Israel was under siege. Ben-Hadad, King of Aram, had mobilized his entire army and marched against Israel, eventually laying siege to Samaria, the capital city of Israel at the time. The siege had been running for many months and there was a severe famine in the city as the Arameans had cut off the food supplies. People were even resorting to eating animals that had been declared unclean by the Jewish law. A donkey head was selling for around two pounds of silver and a cup of seed pods for two ounces of silver. People were literally dying of starvation.

As Joram, the King of Israel, was walking the walls of the city one day he was confronted by a woman who pleaded with him to help her. The story that she told was unbelievably tragic. She was so desperately hungry that she had made an agreement with her friend that she would kill her son and they would eat him, and then her friend would kill her son

41

and they would eat him as well. The woman went on to explain that after they had killed, cooked and eaten her son, her friend had reneged on their agreement and had hidden her son and would not give him up for them to eat.

On hearing this story, the king was so distraught he tore his clothes—a traditional custom expressing absolute despair and grief. The people of Samaria had become so desperate that they had resorted to cannibalism to survive.

It is in the context of this horrible situation recorded in 2 Kings that we find the story of four lepers who were living outside the wall of Samaria during the time of the Aramean siege.[43]

When people in Israel were diagnosed with leprosy they were immediately "cast out." They became known as "unclean" and had to leave their family and home and find whatever habitation they could outside their local community. They scrounged and begged for food and survived as best they could. The Arameans would have had no interest in four lepers who were camping outside the walls of the city; in fact they would have kept as far away from them as possible from fear of contracting the disease themselves.

As the siege progressed and the famine in the city became more severe, less and less food was available for the lepers in the refuse thrown from the city walls. The four lepers reasoned among themselves that they could do one of two things: remain outside the city walls and starve to death, or go down to the Aramean camp and see if they could scrounge or beg some food from the soldiers. They figured that there was a risk the Arameans would kill them, but they would die anyway from hunger if they remained where they were. So they headed off to the Aramean camp.

What they found astounded them. The camp was deserted! It was as though the Arameans had suddenly vanished, leaving all their possessions, food, valuables and animals. In 2 Kings 7 we find the reason why the Arameans had disappeared. We are told that in answer to the prayer of some faithful believers in the city of Samaria, "the Lord had caused the Arameans to hear the sound of chariots and horses and a great army, so that they said to one another, 'Look, the king of Israel has hired the Hittite and Egyptian kings to attack us!'"[44] In fear for their lives the Arameans had fled the camp leaving everything behind.

The lepers were ecstatic. They ran from one tent to another, gorging themselves on all the food, grabbing as many valuables as they could carry and hiding them outside the camp, making many return trips to add to their hoard. As they sat together celebrating their good fortune one of their number observed, "We're not doing right. This is a day of good news and we are keeping it to ourselves. If we wait until daylight, punishment will overtake us. Let's go at once and report this to the royal palace."[45]

When they arrived at the gates of Samaria with their story, they were received with much skepticism. King Joram suspected that the Arameans were in hiding, trying to lure him and his people out of the city so they could ambush them. But the lepers were convincing enough for the king to at least send a scouting party.

The scouting party found all the evidence they needed; the Arameans had indeed fled their camp leaving everything behind. They reported back to the king, and the people poured out of the city gates and plundered the camp. The lepers' "good news" had saved the people of the city of Samaria.

Sharing the Good News

Like the lepers, followers of Jesus have life-saving "good news" that they can either choose to share with others or keep to themselves. The word *gospel* is used throughout the New Testament and literally means "good news." The gospel is the good news about Jesus' life, ministry, teachings, death, resurrection and way of salvation. It is the message that Jesus has entrusted to us to share with the world, and it has the power to transform lives—to take people from a state of spiritual starvation and ultimate "eternal death" to a state of fullness of life, life that can only be found in a relationship with Jesus.

So what are those of us who are of the Kingdom doing with this life-saving message that Jesus has entrusted to us? Are we keeping it to ourselves, plundering the treasures of God's Kingdom with little regard to the ravenous masses who daily cannibalize each other relationally, emotionally and materially, desperately trying to sate their God-sized hunger?

In a video podcast circulating the internet, outspoken atheist Penn Jillette reflects on his reaction to a man who gave him a Bible after one of his shows.[46] Penn—whose car license plates read "atheist," "nogod," and "godless"[47]—expressed a surprising perspective about his encounter with this follower of Jesus. Penn relates how this man came up to him after his show and handed him a Bible. The man explained, "I wrote in the front of it, and I wanted you to have this, I'm kind of proselytizing." Penn spends some time pointing out that this man was not an eccentric weirdo or some kind of religious fanatic, but was a businessman and a genuinely "nice guy," who was both respectful and complimentary about his show.

As he reflects on this encounter, Penn poses the question, "If you believe that there is a heaven and hell, and people could be going to hell, or not getting eternal life, and you think it is not worth telling them this because it would make it socially awkward . . . how much do you have to hate somebody to not proselytize? How much do you have to hate somebody to believe that everlasting life is possible and not tell them that?" Penn then uses the analogy of someone in peril of being hit by a truck, stating that, "If I believed, beyond a shadow of a doubt, that a truck was coming at you and you didn't believe it . . . there is a certain point where I would tackle you, where I would push you out of the way of the truck." Penn then observes that belief in God and heaven and hell is far more important than the truck scenario, because it has to do with eternity.

Penn concludes the podcast by saying, "This guy was a really good guy. He was polite and honest and sane. And he cared enough about me to proselytize, and give me a Bible, which had written in it a little note to me . . . and then five phone numbers and an email address if I wanted to get in touch. Now, I know there is no God, and one polite person living his life right doesn't change that . . . but I tell you, he was a very, very, very good man."

Do we need an atheist to explain to us the compelling reasons that we should share the good news with those who don't know Jesus? Is our compassion for others so overwhelming that we are driven to provide an opportunity for everyone in our circle of influence and beyond to know Jesus and experience eternal life? Or are we so indifferent to others that we don't feel any compulsion to share news that will save them from a lost eternity?

The Apostle Paul said that knowing the power of the Gospel message to save, he was compelled by Christ's love to share the good news with others: "For Christ's love compels us, because we are convinced that one died for all, and therefore all died. And he died for all, that those who live should no longer live for themselves but for him who died for them and was raised again."[48]

Wisely making the most of opportunities

In Ephesians 5:15–16 we are told, "Be very careful, then, how you live—not as unwise but as wise, making the most of every opportunity, because the days are evil." And Colossians 4:5 says, "Be wise in the way you act toward outsiders; make the most of every opportunity."

While sharing the gospel with others is mandated by Jesus,[49] doing it "wisely" in response to the opportunities that God provides is an essential part of the evangelism equation. Untold damage has been done throughout the history of the Church because of unwise, misdirected evangelical zeal.

Rather than "forcing" the gospel on others we need to ask God to provide opportunities to share the good news, trusting him to prepare the way and direct our steps. Convincing people to follow Jesus is the work of the Holy Spirit;[50] our responsibility is to spread the good news,[51] not to coerce people into the Kingdom. However, we need to be prepared to speak when God directs, when the door of opportunity opens to us. In 1 Peter 3:15 we are told to "always be prepared to give an answer to everyone who asks you to give the reason for the hope that you have. But do this with gentleness and respect."

Hunting down unbelievers, shooting evangelical bullets at all who come within our sights, is not consistent with the ethos and calling of Jesus. Often driven by guilt, we find ourselves compelled to "witness," to "tell" others about Jesus, irrespective of whether they are ready to receive the message or not. A far better way is to rely on the direction and leading of the Holy Spirit, looking for those whom God identifies as open to the Gospel; for those needing our love, care, acceptance and respect. We should enter the world each day alert and ready, expressing Jesus in the way we live, trusting God to provide opportunities for us to share the good news.

The man who approached Penn Jillette was making the most of the opportunity available to him. He was a fan of Penn, attending a number of shows as part of his studio audience; and because of his alertness to the opportunities that God provides, he was ready to share the gospel with someone who clearly did not have a relationship with Jesus. His willingness to sensitively, wisely, but courageously step out for Jesus led him to act appropriately in sharing the good news with a man who was a staunch atheist and a champion of the atheist cause. I believe he was well received by Penn for two reasons; first, because God's Spirit was directing him and had prepared the way; and second, because of his pure motives—his genuine love and care for Penn.

Time and again, as we read of Jesus' encounters with various people, we see how he approached them in many different ways. For instance, he took a completely different approach to the Samaritan woman[52]—who was a serial adulterer and from an ethnic group that hated the Jews—than he did with Nicodemus,[53] a Jewish religious leader. Respecting the beliefs and worldview of those we are called to reach and responding accordingly is a characteristic of Jesus that should be evident in our interactions with those outside of the Kingdom.[54]

The caring and sensitive act of the man who approached Penn Jillette and gave him a Bible also opened the door of opportunity for others to be exposed to the gospel. The comments made by thousands who viewed this podcast convey much about the power of the gospel to impact many when it is shared appropriately and under the direction of the Holy Spirit. Penn's musings generated healthy discussion, and in some cases a change of heart, among those who commented on his podcast, both Christians and atheists. Here are a few of the comments:

> I'm an agnostic and I've seen this video before, I just kinda wanted to say that I used to really hate it when people tried to push religion on me, but this really changed the way I look at it.

> ... this video sparked a revelation in our church's youth.

> If you've not seen this, it's an important video no matter what you believe.

When the gospel is shared appropriately, it generates many more opportunities for others to be exposed to the good news.

Preaching the Gospel

Sharing the gospel with those who don't know Jesus is

intrinsically tied to the advancement of God's Kingdom.[55] Jesus defined his mission as being to "preach the good news of the kingdom of God," declaring that this was the reason he was sent to our world.[56] If this was Jesus' mission, then as followers of Jesus, it has to be ours as well.

In Mark 16:15 Jesus commands his disciples to "Go into all the world and preach the good news to all creation." The word *preach* conveys the concept of declaration, advocacy and explanation. Preaching can occur in a variety of contexts, from one-on-one interaction through proclamation to large gatherings. Collectively and individually we have been commissioned by Jesus to advance his Kingdom by proactively engaging in the declaration of the gospel.

So what does this proclamation of the gospel look like in a world where the church is constantly—with some justification—accused of being far too "preachy"? Is it still valid to openly and simply share the gospel message with others? Is there still a place for "proclamation evangelism"? I believe there is, if it is done in the context of meaningful and loving relationship.

Providing people with an opportunity to be followers of Jesus is one of the primary responsibilities of citizens of the Kingdom of God. Knowing the eternal implications of not having a relationship with Jesus, and driven by a desire that others don't miss out on all the wonder and blessings of the Kingdom of God, followers of Jesus should be compelled to share the gospel story with all in their circle of influence.

Of course, one of the most effective ways to present the gospel and offer people an opportunity to become followers of Jesus is "one-on-one," naturally sharing the story of Jesus in the context of loving relationship. But not all are confident or feel competent in presenting the gospel or challenging people to give their life to Jesus in large-group settings. The benefit of being part of the Kingdom is that there are members of the Kingdom who have the gift of evangelism and are especially called and equipped by God to "preach the gospel"—to share the good news in a public forum.

Having gifted communicators of the gospel in the context of a community of believers allows all members of God's family to participate in the "preaching" of the good news. Local churches and Christian organizations drawing on the giftedness of evangelists in the Church can provide opportunities for followers of Jesus to share the gospel with those in their circle of influence. In fact, I believe it is a responsibility of local church communities to plan, organize and provide regular events, programs, small groups, activities and services to which members of their community can invite friends knowing they will be presented with the gospel and be provided with an opportunity to respond.

Providing people who don't know Jesus with an opportunity to be exposed to public preaching of the good news by gifted preachers and evangelists is a legitimate and biblically supported means of sharing the gospel. However, the effectiveness of the public presentation of the gospel is very much dependent upon the quality of relationship that those who are being exposed to the gospel have developed with a follower or followers of Jesus. If you are truly representing Jesus to the people in your circle of influence, they will be far more likely to join you at an event or gathering where they can find out more about Jesus; and they will certainly be more open and responsive to an invitation to become a follower of Jesus. If you are not already "living Jesus" in all arenas of your life, and suddenly start asking your acquaintances and friends to come to an outreach event where they can hear about Jesus, the response is probably not going to be very positive.

Proclamation in a relational context

As a leader in Youth for Christ I have been involved in many "evangelism events." At all the youth meetings, concerts, rallies, festivals and camps that I have participated in, almost without exception, when young people have responded to a gospel appeal they have been brought to the event by other young people. It is because of a relationship with followers of Jesus that these young people are exposed to Jesus and respond to the gospel. The event is just the "reaping ground," a culmination of an extensive period of "relational evangelism." It is also in the context of a personal relationship with followers of Jesus that those who respond to an "invitation" at an event are followed up and discipled.

A ministry colleague was asked to speak at a youth convention in a South Asian Islamic nation. In the final program he presented a simple gospel message and at the end of his message invited young people to respond. Quite a number of those present indicated that they wanted to become followers of Jesus. Each of them was then paired up with volunteers and staff running the event to ensure they understood what was involved in being a follower of Jesus.

As my colleague watched young people talking and praying together, he felt someone touching his feet—which were bare due to the cultural requirement of removing footwear when in a dwelling or building. He looked down to see a girl kneeling before him, crying and wiping her tears off his feet with her hair. Feeling very uncomfortable and concerned about the girl's behavior, my colleague immediately called over one of the leaders and asked her to talk to the girl.

After an animated conversation with the girl, the leader explained to my colleague that this girl had for several years been sharing her faith with her friend. She had invited her friend to the event, and her friend had been one of the young people who had responded to the invitation to become a follower of Jesus. This girl was so overwhelmed with love for her friend that it spilled out in this amazing display of gratitude to the person who had been the instrument by which her friend had been brought into a relationship with Jesus. Jesus was so much a part of this girl's life that she radiated his compassion for the "lost." My colleague realized that his preaching and invitation was just the final step in a long relational process, and that the primary reason for her friend's response to the appeal was the girl's love and prayers for her and her authentic expression of Jesus in their day-to-day interactions.

A deep Jesus-driven love for others, coupled with a clear explanation of the gospel, is the most effective form of evangelism.

The Power of the Gospel

A number of years ago, while visiting the Youth for Christ ministry leaders in Nepal, I was asked by the National Director to speak at a youth outreach event. We travelled for many hours to a remote township where the local Youth for

Christ leaders had gathered together around three hundred young people for a regional youth festival.

After some fun activities and a very lively concert by the Nepal Youth for Christ band, I was asked to speak to the young people attending the event. With the help of an interpreter I gave a message about friends, specifically focusing upon Jesus as being the greatest friend anyone could have, explaining as simply as I could the gospel story. At the conclusion of my message I asked if anyone would like to have Jesus as their friend, and if they did, to indicate this by putting up their hand. Nearly every hand in the room went up.

I was very concerned. Clearly these young people did not understand what I was asking of them. I told them to put their hands down. I explained in a lot more detail what it meant to give your life to Jesus. I talked more about Jesus' identity and what was involved in being a follower of him. I then asked for the second time who would like to "give their life to Jesus." Nearly all the hands went up again!

Deeply perturbed by this, I asked my interpreter to explain in his own words what I was asking, to help me out by telling these young people the implications of being a follower of Jesus. The interpreter spoke for a few minutes and then looked to me for further instructions. Once again I asked who would like to give their life to Jesus. The same number of hands went up.

I couldn't believe it. Most of these young people were from Hindu families and I expected that they didn't know a lot about Jesus. Surely not all these three hundred plus young people were "getting it." Were they really all genuinely giving their lives over to Jesus? But I had done my best to explain the gospel. So I closed the meeting in prayer, specifically praying for all these new followers of Jesus.

After the close of the program I immediately went and
found Nico, the National Director of Youth for Christ in
Nepal. I asked him whether he thought I had been clear
in presenting the gospel. He said that he thought it was a
very simple and powerful gospel message. I then asked him
whether he thought that all those who indicated they were
committing their life to Jesus fully understood what they were
doing. His response was, "I believe that most knew exactly
what they were doing. But what you need to understand,
David, is that all of these young people were brought to this
event by one of the Youth for Christ staff or volunteers, and
every one of them who made a commitment tonight will be
followed up and discipled by those who brought them."

In Romans 1:16 Paul says, "I am not ashamed of the
gospel, because it is the power of God for the salvation of
everyone who believes." The gospel, when it is faithfully,
authentically and clearly presented has enormous power to
change lives. When in Nepal, I underestimated the power of
the gospel. I didn't believe that it could impact so many in
such a way that they would all be drawn to Jesus and genuinely
desire to give their lives over to him. Never underestimate
the transformational power of the gospel. Of course, my
Nepal experience also reinforced the importance of personal
relational "evangelism" as foundational to the efficacy of public
gospel presentation. All of these young people who came to
Jesus had already experienced Jesus to some degree in their
relationship with the Youth for Christ staff and volunteers.

Providing an Opportunity for
Others to Follow Jesus

What does it mean to provide people with a legitimate
"opportunity" to be a follower of Jesus? In the context of the

Great Commission,[57] clearly this is a question that needs to be answered for all who follow Jesus. We are asked by Jesus to provide an opportunity for all in the world to know him. What does it mean to "preach the gospel" to all humankind? When have we fulfilled the mandate to share the good news with others?

In Youth for Christ we have three qualitative measures that are applied to all of our youth ministry programs in assessing their effectiveness and relevance:

1. Can all young people who have been through the program provide a legitimate and accurate answer to the question "do you know who Jesus is?"

2. Do all of the young people who have been through the program know how to enter into a relationship with Jesus if they choose to do so?

3. Are all the young people who have been through the program able to identify YFC staff and/or volunteers who they could turn to if they have a problem or are in trouble?

These three questions are the qualifiers for any specific Youth for Christ program or ministry strategy. Our desire is to do everything possible to provide young people with an opportunity to be followers of Jesus. If these three questions cannot all be answered in the affirmative for a Youth for Christ program or process, then we are not making the most of the opportunity to introduce young people to Jesus, and we need to either modify or discard the program.

All followers of Jesus have been given their marching

orders to make the most of every opportunity to represent Jesus,[58] share his love,[59] preach the gospel[60] and make disciples.[61] If we claim to be citizens of the Kingdom of God, applying the above qualifying questions to our "circle of influence" relationships would be a valid way of assessing whether we are effectively making the most of the opportunities available to us to share Jesus with others. So let me rephrase these questions in the context of the Kingdom imperative to preach the good news to all humankind:

1. Can all the people in your circle of influence give a legitimate and accurate answer when asked the question "do you know who Jesus is?"

2. Do all the people in your circle of influence know how to enter into a relationship with Jesus if they choose to do so?

3. Would all the people in your circle of influence feel welcome to approach you if they have a problem or are in trouble? Do they know or believe that you care for them—that you love them unconditionally?

Working toward an affirmative answer to all these questions I believe would enable followers of Jesus to be more open, caring and intentional in their relationships with others, and greatly increase their capacity to draw those in their circle of influence into a relationship with Jesus.

An "Informed" Decision

The other element of the Youth for Christ vision that requires some explanation is the term "informed decision." Providing people with an opportunity to make an informed decision to be a follower of Jesus is the key to making disciples rather than merely converts. The great commission of Jesus to all who would follow him was to "go and make disciples of all nations, baptizing them in the name of the Father and of the Son and of the Holy Spirit, and teaching them to obey everything I have commanded you."[62]

Unfortunately, the enormousness of this task, along with the urgency implied in the command, can tend to drive Christians to engage in practices and activities designed to get as many as possible, in the shortest time possible, to make a decision to become followers of Christ. I have been at several events where young people have been manipulated to "give their life to Jesus." When I have had the opportunity to connect with these young people after the event, they generally have little or no understanding of what it actually means to be a follower of Jesus.

I have a friend whose father was an itinerant preacher. He recalls being at a convention where a number of speakers were preaching, including his father. As each speaker came to the backstage area after delivering a message they would literally "boast" about how many responses they received to their appeal. They ended each day with a meeting of all the speakers where they tallied up the number who "gave their lives to Jesus," each hoping to be the one who got the most "decisions."

Jesus doesn't call his followers to seek "converts" to Christianity. He calls us to introduce others to him—to offer people the opportunity to be his disciples. Conversion is a religious concept. Following Jesus is all about relationship, not religion. Jesus didn't create a new religion or call people to become part of a religious sect or community; he simply asked people to "follow" him; he invited them into relationship with him.

There are many examples in the Bible of Jesus explaining to people the implications of joining him, before inviting them to become one of his followers. In Mark 10 we read of a rich young man who approached Jesus and asked him what was involved in being part of his Kingdom and securing eternal life. Obviously he asked this question in the context of knowing who Jesus was and being attracted to him. Jesus explained that following him would cost everything, that to be his follower this young man would need to give up everything he treasured in his life. On being informed of what was involved in following Jesus, the young man decided he couldn't do it; it was just too costly for him. He made an "informed decision" not to follow Jesus.

Another example of a person who was well informed about Jesus and the gospel prior to being challenged to become a follower is found in Acts 26. Paul is brought before King Agrippa and gives a lengthy explanation of what it means to be a disciple of Jesus, referring to the king's prior knowledge of Jesus' teachings, death and resurrection. Paul shared with the king the story of how he met Jesus and became one of his disciples, and the impact this had on his life. As in the case of the rich young man, when confronted with the implications of following Jesus, Agrippa was not prepared to become one of his followers. He also made an "informed decision."

In Acts 2 we are told how Peter stands before a large crowd, preaches the gospel, and invites people to give their life to Jesus. But Peter does this in the context of the people's personal experience of Jesus.[63] Referring to Jesus' life, death and resurrection Peter challenges people to consider following Jesus in the light of what they know, have seen, and now understand. On this occasion three thousand made an "informed decision" to follow Jesus.

Striving to get people to simply "make decisions" is not consistent with the great commission's imperative to "make disciples." The very word *disciple* implies an intimate knowledge of—and an absolute commitment to—the one being followed. If we are serious about making disciples, then we will inform people thoroughly of what following Jesus involves before asking them to consider following him. People need to know who Jesus is and the implications of being a follower of Jesus before they can genuinely consider handing their life over to him. They need to make an "informed" decision because being a disciple of Jesus impacts every aspect of this life and the life beyond. It is a "life and death" decision, and should not be entered into without careful consideration.

Jesus said the greatest commandments were to love God with all our heart, soul, mind and strength and to love our neighbor as we love ourselves.[64] If we follow Jesus and believe that he is the source of life and love both now and into eternity, then how can we withhold the truth of the gospel from our neighbor? Surely, sharing Jesus with our neighbors—our friends, family and acquaintances—would be the ultimate expression of our love for God and our love and care for our neighbors.

CHAPTER 3

When the Kingdom Comes . . .

PEOPLE WILL BE BLESSED, BELONG, BELIEVE AND BECOME

Now the tax collectors and "sinners" were all gathering around to hear him. But the Pharisees and the teachers of the law muttered, "This man welcomes sinners and eats with them."
(Luke 15:1–2)

A number of years ago a suburb in the city of Rotterdam in the Netherlands was declared by the government as a "no-go" zone for the police. Populated by Dutch Antilles refugees, the area had become so violent and out-of-control that it was unsafe for police to venture there alone or in small numbers.

About a year after this declaration two young men, Setkin and Daniel, who worked with Youth for Christ in the Netherlands, approached their national director, Edward, with what seemed like a crazy idea. They told him that they had been praying about the situation in Rotterdam and felt that God was calling them to establish a ministry in the Dutch Antillean community. They wanted to go into the "no-go" area and try to set up a youth center. So compelling was their vision and call that Edward finally agreed to let them at least investigate the possibility of establishing a ministry in this hostile and needy community.

Fueled by a calling and passion for the Antillean young people, these courageous young men went into the area and somehow managed to connect with representatives of the local community. They told them they were with Youth for Christ and that they wanted to set up a youth center to serve and care for young people. The response to their request was disappointing. They were told that Christians were not welcome, that Christians had visited the area in the past, and all they had done was "Preach at us, told us we were going to hell, and then left without helping the community in any way at all."

Undaunted by this disheartening news, Daniel and Setkin said they were different, they were there to stay. In fact, they said they would move into the area with their wives. They also made a promise to the community representatives that they would not "preach." They said they would simply serve the community in any way they could—and that is exactly what they did.

They moved into the area with their wives. They were given the use of an old abandoned government building that was being used by crack dealers to cook cocaine. They cleaned the building and set up a small youth center. The building was constantly vandalized. Threats of violence were common. But these young men and their wives persevered. They loved and served the local community without preaching at them— providing a place for young people to hang out, inviting people to their homes, serving and meeting the needs of the people.

After about two years one of the local gang leaders came to

them and told them he and some of his friends wanted to know more about this Jesus that they served. Setkin and Daniel told this young man that they would be happy to share more about Jesus and invited him to come to the youth center on Thursday evening. Around fifty young people turned up, including the gang leader and forty members of his gang. Setkin and Daniel had invited an Antillean who had found Jesus while in prison to come and share his story. After this man told the group how Jesus had changed his life, Setkin and Daniel explained who Jesus was and what it meant to be a follower of him.

When Setkin and Daniel had finished sharing, the local gang leader who had requested the meeting jumped to his feet and addressing his gang members stated, "We need to do this; we need to give our lives to Jesus." Daniel tried to discourage them from taking this step, because he thought they must have misunderstood what it meant to be a follower of Jesus. But they insisted that they all wanted to make a commitment to follow Jesus, declaring they knew exactly what they were doing. And so that night, an Antillean gang leader and forty members of his gang surrendered their lives to Jesus.

The community was transformed. More young people started coming to the youth center, invited by the core group of former gang members who were now followers of Jesus. Additional staff were recruited, including many volunteers from churches in the Rotterdam area. Community programs were developed that served single mothers, drug users, illiterate young people and victims of rape and abuse.

Setkin and Daniel now have a thriving youth ministry reaching many young people in the area. The youth center has been expanded to include a woodworking area in which young people are trained in carpentry and furniture manufacture. There is a room full of computers in which young people learn computer skills. Christian business men and women mentor young people, helping them to establish small business ventures, sometimes even providing loans.

The crime rate in the area has gone down 70 percent. The police have assigned a full-time police woman to work with Youth for Christ in serving and liaising with the local community leaders. It is now safe for anyone to enter the area, including the police and government workers.

At the request of the Antillean community a church has been established and is currently being pastored by Daniel. The church was named "Thugz Church" by the Antillean young people, alluding to a song titled *Thugz Mansion* by popular rapper 2Pac, which is about life after death and heaven for criminals. The young people said they chose the name "because it tells everyone that they are welcome. It doesn't matter what you have done. God loves you and wants to give you a new start."

Cultural Christianity: Believe, Behave, Belong

Through the love, care and acceptance of Setkin and Daniel the Antillean people found a place in God's Kingdom. Setkin and Daniel created a "Kingdom community" that was solely designed to bless the Antilleans, and when they encountered this community, these lost and hurting people immediately felt they belonged. They were welcome as they were; and it was in the context of the Kingdom community that the Antilleans encountered Jesus and progressively discovered what it meant to be a follower of him.

Unfortunately, in many established local churches today, the process of becoming a part of the church community is for someone to first *believe* in a prescribed set of doctrinal and theological precepts; then *behave* in accordance with the "norms" of the community; and then they can *belong* by being validated by the leaders of the church as being in compliance with the beliefs and behavioral expectations of the community. When the institutional norms of a church or denomination—which are generally tied to subculture values—become the primary definers of acceptability and "belongingness," a cultural Christianity emerges. Cultural Christianity is one of the greatest impediments to the advancement of the Kingdom of God in the world today.

People who are not familiar with a highly organized and narrowly defined expression of local church find it very hard to relate to the culture of the church and struggle to fit in. Not only are these local churches unattractive to those outside the Church, but they also seem to eventually repel many within the church itself. This is supported by the significant decline in attendance numbers of mainline institutionalized churches globally, particularly in Western society.[65]

Brian Fulthrop, commenting on the dramatic decline of church attendance among Anglicans-Episcopalians in North America states:

> So it is true that how we do church does need
> to be somewhat re-evaluated. Probably we need
> more organic church than institutionalized
> church—as once a church (the local church or
> the denomination) becomes too institutionalized,

it automatically stops growing. Institutionalism
tends to come as a result of losing focus (which
can tend to focus on maintaining an organization
and its structures over winning the lost and
engaging a lost world).[66]

Forcing Christianity into a systematized set of behavioral
expectations and cultural norms fosters "religion," which
focuses upon form and function rather than nurturing a
relationship with Jesus. Cultural Christianity works against an
authentic experience of Jesus and his transformational power.
Controlling the outcomes of a person's encounter with God
produces a contrived and prescriptive religious environment
that is defined by the cultural values and worldview of the
"stakeholders" of the community, rather than the Holy
Spirit. In this religious environment, outsiders—including
unbelievers—simply don't feel they belong.

James Hudson Taylor was one of the most innovative and
revolutionary cross-cultural missionaries in the history of the
Church. However, Hudson Taylor's initial foray into China
in 1853 was not very successful. He was sent by a mission
society that had a cultural Christianity approach to ministry,
mission and church. The view at the time was that when
heathens converted to Christianity, they would indicate the
genuine nature of their conversion by becoming "civilized."
They were expected to dress in the Western clothing style of
the missionary, and as the numbers of converts increased, they
were encouraged to build a church mimicking the architecture
of the church buildings "back home." In church services the
converts sang hymns and followed liturgy prescribed by the
sending church or mission organization.

After struggling for a number of years with little mission success and battling theft and loss of all his possessions, serious illness and alienation by the local people, Hudson Taylor stumbled across a new way to do mission. Due to his desperate circumstance he was forced to live with the people. He began to dress in the local clothing, grew his hair long and plaited it in a pigtail down his back, grew a moustache and little beard, and overall embraced the Chinese culture.

As Hudson Taylor became more proficient in Mandarin and immersed himself in the local community he was able to "live Jesus" among the people, and as the people encountered Jesus in the context of their culture, they too wanted to become his followers. Many joined Taylor as followers of Jesus, and eventually the local believers formed a church and started worshiping in a style appropriate to their culture.

After several years the mission society sent someone to investigate the work of Hudson Taylor. They were horrified. They reported back to headquarters that Hudson Taylor had "gone native." They tried to recall him but he would not leave, so they disowned him. Although this deeply troubled Taylor at the time, it was ultimately a great blessing in that it freed him from the structures and restrictions of the institutionalized church and mission society.

During his fifty-one years of missionary service, Taylor established the China Inland Mission (CIM), was responsible for bringing around eight hundred missionaries to China (including unmarried women, which no one had done before) and, along with his fellow workers, was credited with leading more than thirty thousand Chinese nationals to Christ by the time he died at age seventy-three.

Unfortunately, many institutionalized churches today have similar expectations to those of the mission society that originally sent Hudson Taylor to China. They expect people to fit rigidly defined cultural norms to belong, and people who don't comply with these cultural expectations don't have a place in the church.

Cultural expectations often include the way people dress, their political affiliation, their ethnicity, their musical tastes, their economic status and their educational standard. Along with these cultural compliances, certain behaviors are also expected for people to be accepted by the church community. For example, use of colorful language, sporadic attendance of church services, identification with a political figure or party, and use of alcohol or tobacco products often define people "out." Agreement with a particular theology and religious praxis, formal commitment to membership, monetary contribution, and attendance at various events and services of the church define people "in."

In my earlier book *The Next Wave* I told a story that is very relevant to this discussion of alienation and rejection due to cultural expectations of a church.[67] The story relates to an experience I had when I was a teenager growing up in a conservative church in the northern suburbs of Melbourne, Australia. At our request, the youth group leaders had arranged a meeting with the church eldership to allow a number of us to present our concerns to the elders. There was a rising level of discontent in the youth community over the lack of cultural relevance of the church to our peers, and some of us in the youth group were advocating change so that we could more effectively reach our friends and integrate them into the church.

At the meeting we were given the opportunity to put our case to the elders. One of my closest friends spoke up first, and in trying to explain the challenges we were facing in bridging the cultural divide, stated that he would be "embarrassed" to bring one of his unchurched friends to an outreach service, because the services were so conservative and alien to the youth culture in which he lived. Before he could say any more, one of the elders jumped to his feet, and in an angry voice and with an accusing finger pointing at my friend, stated, "How dare you say you are ashamed of your faith." He then quoted Mark 8:38, which says, "Whosoever therefore shall be ashamed of me and of my words in this adulterous and sinful generation; of him also shall the Son of man be ashamed, when he cometh in the glory of his Father with the holy angels."[68] He proceeded with a barrage of criticism of youth in general, lecturing us all on what he saw as a weakness of faith that had resulted in us "selling out" to the world and compromising our "witness" by trying to incorporate the world's corrupt culture into the church.

I watched as my friend visibly wilted under this barrage of unexpected and vitriolic criticism. This elder had completely dismissed the validity of our youth culture because it didn't align with his version of Christianity. Blinded by his own cultural narrow-mindedness, he was unable to see the passion and love that this young man had for his lost friends. The message conveyed was that my friend and I, and the other representatives of the youth who were attending this meeting, didn't "belong" in the church. My friend's innocent and simple faith was severely shaken. He walked out of the church that day and, as far as I know, never entered a church again.

Un-Christian

Serving in an international ministry leadership role requires that I travel to many places around the world and meet many people from a wide range of ethnic, social, economic and religious backgrounds. Over the past few years, as I have been introduced into new social networks, I have become progressively more reluctant to identify myself as a Christian, because there are now so many negative connotations and stereotypes associated with the word. Unfortunately, the word *Christian* in many cultural and societal contexts no longer conveys the values of the Kingdom of God, the nature of Jesus, and the all-embracing invitation of the Gospel. Instead, Christianity is often associated with Western culture, conservative politics, fundamentalism, judgmentalism, arrogance, materialism, hypocrisy, exclusivism and superiority. To avoid confusion, prejudgment and sometimes outright hostility, rather than using "Christian" to describe who I am, I find it more appropriate to refer to myself as a "follower of Jesus."

In their groundbreaking book *UnChristian,* authors David Kinnaman and Gabe Lyons reported on a major research project that investigated the perceptions about Christians within the general population in the United States. In the book they described the increasingly negative reputation of Christians, especially among young people. The research convincingly shows that Christians are now best known for what they are against. They are perceived as being hypocritical, insincere, concerned only with "converting" others, anti-homosexual, sheltered, too political and judgmental. Young people are especially quick to point out that Christianity today seems to have little relationship with what Jesus intended it to be.

Throughout the book the authors quoted people they surveyed to illustrate what the research was unveiling. The following quotes are two poignant examples:

> Everyone in my church gave me advice about how to raise my son, but a lot of times they seemed to be reminding me that I have no husband—and besides, most of them were not following their own advice. It made it hard to care about what they said. They were not practicing what they preached.

> Victoria, 24[69]

> Christians talk about hating sin and loving sinners, but the way they go about things, they might as well call it what it is. They hate the sin *and* the sinner.

> Jeff, 25[70]

The authors concluded that Christians are known as un-Christian because:

> The church has lost its ability and willingness to love and accept people who are not part of the "insider" club. This failure is draining the vigor from our faith. We say we love outsiders, but

in many cases we show love only if it is on our
terms, if they are interested in coming to our
church, or if they respect our way of life.

We want young generations to participate in
our churches, but we expect them to play by the
rules, look the part, embrace the music, and use
the right language.[71]

In many ways institutional Christianity has become a
religion that is "counter-dependent," deriving its identity by
what it stands against. I often hear fellow believers declaring
that we have to take a stand, that we have to declare that
we are against this or that, and that we have to fight for our
moral and ethical position. People who don't align well with
the declared position—particularly political and religious
leaders—are seen as the enemy and are regularly demonized.
I have met many Christians who have told me that they are
praying for the demise of political leaders; in one case a woman
declared that she was praying and hoping that the leader of
her nation would be "taken out" (assassinated). I constantly
receive emails from Christian friends and acquaintances
lampooning and attacking the character of individuals who
they feel don't align with their politicized Christian values,
often manipulating and misrepresenting the "facts" to support
their attack.

In an investigation conducted in the United States by
Barna researchers, two open-ended questions were asked of a
large sample of people from the general public: "What were
Christians' recent positive contributions and what were the
negative ones?"

"Overall," researchers noted, "there was a more extensive and diverse list of complaints about Christians and their churches than there was of examples of the benefits they have provided to society."[72] At the top of the negatives list: One in five Americans, or 20 percent, said Christians have incited violence or hatred in the name of Jesus Christ. Of the non-Christians surveyed, 35 percent gave this response. One in four Americans said they couldn't think of a single positive societal contribution made by Christians in recent years.

If Christians are known as uncaring, critical, isolationist, politically polarizing, hateful people, then it is little wonder that people outside the Church perceive the Church as a judgmental and unwelcoming community. This positioning of the Church does not represent Jesus well, nor does it reflect the values of his Kingdom.

Rather than being known for what they are against, followers of Jesus should be known for what they stand for. Jesus was unequivocal in what he stood for, declaring by word and deed a new way for humankind that did away with the old system of retribution, legalism, exclusivism and domination of others.

If we truly identify with Jesus then we will be people who are known for our unconditional love of others, as those who forgive when retribution is warranted, seek peace when others want to fight, and stand for the truth even when it is unpopular to do so. We will be known for our generosity, kindness, humility, unselfishness and sacrificial giving to those in need. We will welcome those whom others reject, defend the defenseless and alienated, and seek justice for all.

Jesus overwhelmed people with love, accepting and

welcoming those the religious system rejected. He was criticized for being a friend of sinners[73]—for including people in his Kingdom who didn't "make the grade" in the organized religious systems of the Jewish community.

Jesus' followers should be known for the same things for which Jesus was known. If Jesus was known as "a friend of sinners," so should we. A church community that epitomizes Jesus will be a place where all feel welcome—a place where "sinners" are loved and feel that they belong and have a valid role and place in the community.

Kingdom Encounter: Bless, Belong, Believe and Become

As opposed to the "believe, behave, belong" rite of passage of cultural Christianity, I am convinced that when people encounter an authentic Kingdom community they will first be uniquely *blessed*. Then as they are unconditionally embraced by the church community they will feel that they have a place in the community—that they *belong*. Through their interaction with followers of Jesus they will personally encounter Jesus and have an opportunity to *believe* in him and wholeheartedly begin the journey to *become* all that God has uniquely designed them to be.

Bless, belong, believe and become should be the progressive experience of anyone who encounters a genuine expression of God's Kingdom.

Bless

Most of the remaining chapters of this book are devoted to the subject of blessing others, exploring the calling and challenge to those who follow Jesus to be a blessing to all humankind. There are many ways you can be a blessing to others, both "passive," through the transformative power of the Holy Spirit operating in your life that naturally overflows to those around you, and "active," through a deliberate and intentional response to a specific individual or collective need.

People should be blessed by their encounters with authentic followers of Jesus. If every follower of Jesus began each day asking the Lord to reveal to them someone in need—and then actively journeyed through the day looking for the "someone" to bless—the Kingdom would quickly invade every corner of this earth.

Even something little given or done out of genuine love and compassion can make a huge difference to a person who is struggling to make sense of life, especially those who have become cynical and disillusioned by the individualism and selfishness of those around them. The legendary Greek philosopher Aesop was absolutely right when he said, "No act of kindness, no matter how small, is ever wasted." It is a Kingdom principle that a tiny seed of goodness, love, grace or kindness sown in the world can reap an enormous harvest.[74]

Lana Gates, writing in the Phoenix *Examiner*, shares the following experience of how a little act of kindness significantly impacted her life:

> My husband made our bed this morning. I am in awe. You see, in our 18 years of marriage, I can count on one hand the number of times my husband has done this deed all on his own. There have been many times he's helped me make the bed, but today he did it without my

> knowledge. And that little act of kindness made
> my day!
>
> Why would such a little thing mean so much?
> Because it says to me that my husband was
> thinking of me. He knows I've been busy and
> wanted to do a small thing to help me.[75]

Renowned novelist and historian Charles Kingsley said, "Make it a rule and pray to God to help you keep it . . . never, if possible, to lie down at night without being able to say 'I have made one human being at least a little wiser, a little happier, or a little better this day.'"

Jesus called us to shine our light in this world,[76] and I believe the way that we best do this is to give unconditionally to others at their point of need. Deliberately looking for the needs of others around us and being prepared to respond to those needs is an essential part of light-shining Kingdom living. Blessing others is the first step of bringing them into the Kingdom.

Belong

The inclusiveness of the gospel

In Ephesians Paul talks of the "great mystery" of the gospel, which he believes was hidden until the coming of Christ and the establishment of his Kingdom.[77] The mystery is so revolutionary that Paul goes to great lengths to explain that this truth was not his idea, but that it has been revealed to him and to the other apostles by a special revelation from God.[78] The mystery is that "the Gentiles" (that is everyone else in the world apart from the Jews) are "fellow heirs," and "members together of one body, and sharers together of the promise in Christ Jesus" through the gospel.[79]

Everyone "belongs"! That is the revolutionary truth of the Gospel of Jesus Christ that Paul revealed in Ephesians. And why did Paul present this as such a revolutionary concept—a concept so hard to accept that he had to emphasize that it was completely God's idea and not his? It was because he was operating in the context of the religious institutions of the Jewish faith, and he knew that this concept would be incredibly difficult for the institutional "gate keepers" to accept or understand.

In any institutional expression of faith it is extremely difficult for those who control the institutions to embrace the concept that all belong. Religious institutions are notoriously exclusive. One of the great mysteries of the Kingdom of God—which flies in the face of organized religion—is the "inclusiveness" of the Gospel. Jesus died for all and therefore all belong in the Kingdom. I am not advocating for "universalism"—it is clear in God's Word that Jesus is the "only way"; that people have to believe in the identity and "truth" of Jesus and commit to follow him to be members of God's family. But it is also clear that the price has been paid and the way made clear for all humanity to have a place in his Kingdom. All are welcome in God's Kingdom and therefore all who encounter the Kingdom should feel they have a place—that they belong in the family; the question is whether or not they will accept the offer of citizenship.

Believe

Follow me . . .

Jesus didn't ask people to convert to an ideology or a religion. He didn't ask people to "become Christians." He simply asked people to follow him. Jesus also didn't impose his way on others; he invited people to join him in his Father's Kingdom:

> "Come, follow me," Jesus said, "and I will make you fishers of men." (Matthew 4:19)

> But Jesus told him, "Follow me, and let the dead bury their own dead." (Matthew 8:22)

> As Jesus went on from there, he saw a man named Matthew sitting at the tax collector's booth. "Follow me," he told him, and Matthew got up and followed him. (Matthew 9:9)

> "Anyone who does not take his cross and follow me is not worthy of me." (Matthew 10:38)

> Then Jesus said to his disciples, "If anyone would come after me, he must deny himself and take up his cross and follow me." (Matthew 16:24)

> Jesus answered, "If you want to be perfect, go, sell your possessions and give to the poor, and you will have treasure in heaven. Then come, follow me." (Matthew 19:21)

"Come, follow me," Jesus said, "and I will make you fishers of men." (Mark 1:17)

As he walked along, he saw Levi son of Alphaeus sitting at the tax collector's booth. "Follow me," Jesus told him, and Levi got up and followed him. (Mark 2:14)

Then he called the crowd to him along with his disciples and said: "If anyone would come after me, he must deny himself and take up his cross and follow me. (Mark 8:34)

Jesus looked at him and loved him. "One thing you lack," he said. "Go, sell everything you have and give to the poor, and you will have treasure in heaven. Then come, follow me." (Mark 10:21)

After this, Jesus went out and saw a tax collector by the name of Levi sitting at his tax booth. "Follow me," Jesus said to him. (Luke 5:27)

Then he said to them all: "If anyone would come after me, he must deny himself and take up his cross daily and follow me." (Luke 9:23)

He said to another man, "Follow me." (Luke 9:59)

"And anyone who does not carry his cross and follow me cannot be my disciple." (Luke 14:27)

> When Jesus heard this, he said to him, "You still
> lack one thing. Sell everything you have and
> give to the poor, and you will have treasure in
> heaven. Then come, follow me." (Luke 18:22)

The early Christians declared themselves to be "followers of the Way" [80] rather than being identified as belonging to a new religion or sect. Jesus was "the Way"[81] and his followers simply committed themselves to following "the way of Jesus." In fact, they still retained their cultural, and in some cases, religious identity. There were Jewish followers of Jesus, Greek followers of Jesus, Arab followers of Jesus, Cretan followers of Jesus.[82] The problems came when the members of one of the cultures imposed their religious practice on others.[83]

If Jesus didn't ask people to convert to a religion or an ideology, then neither should we. Becoming Kingdom citizens has nothing to do with accepting a catalogue of rules or aligning with a religion—it is all about a relationship with Jesus. The mandate of the gospel is to provide people with an opportunity to be followers of Jesus. As citizens of the Kingdom of God our primary task is to introduce people to Jesus, not to try to get them to commit to a religious system called Christianity.

Christianity as a movement

Unraveling the complexities of cultural Christianity, and determining the validity or otherwise of praxis, form and function of the institutional structures and entities of the Church, is not easy. However, I have found that defining the "nature" of the Church is helpful in better understanding healthy form and function of the local church—what we should be inviting people to be a part of.

Steve Addison in his book *Movements that Change the World* makes a strong case for Christianity being a "movement" rather than a religion or an institution. He defines movements as:

> informal groupings of people and organizations pursuing a common cause. They are people with an agenda for change. Movements don't have members, but they do have participants. The goals of a movement can be furthered by organizations, but organizations are not the totality of the movement. A movement can have leading figures, but no one person or group controls a movement. Movements are made up of people who are committed to a common cause.[84]

Rather than viewing Jesus as a founder of a religion, Addison presents Jesus as the founder of a missionary movement: "Jesus was the first missionary. He didn't start an organization, he didn't write a book, and he didn't run for office. What Jesus did was found a missionary movement that would one day span the globe"[85]

It seems to me that the distinction between being part of a movement and being a member of an institutionalized religion is the priority of the commitment. As Addison points out:

> At the beginning of his ministry Jesus proclaimed, "The time has come. The Kingdom

of God is near. Repent and believe the good news!" Jesus' cause was the Kingdom of God. . . . Jesus demonstrated unwavering commitment to his mission. Before launching his public ministry, he won a private battle against Satan's attempts to divert him from the true nature of his mission. He faced the continued scrutiny and opposition of the religious leaders. At the right time, he set his face to go to Jerusalem and die for the cause he championed. He died deserted by his closest companions.

Jesus expected the same unwavering commitment from his disciples. He expected his closest disciples to walk from their livelihoods, to leave their homes behind, and to follow him.

Jesus expected his followers to make the same sacrifices and demonstrate the same commitment that he did. Only those willing to take up their cross and follow him could be his disciples. Their loyalty to him had to come before every other loyalty.[86]

"The cause" of a movement is an all-consuming passion for those who are participants of the movement. It is their preeminent life priority. Movement participants are advocates for the cause in all arenas of life, and anyone who knows them knows what they are passionate about. In contrast, for someone who is a member of an institutionalized religion or a religious organization, particularly in Western society, very often their "religion" is only a part of "what they do," having equal or less priority than the many other things that fill up that person's life. It is important, but it doesn't define who they are.

If we are part of the Kingdom movement, our "cause"— our all-consuming passion—should be Jesus and establishing God's Kingdom on the earth as it is in heaven. Our cause informs who we are, is the primary determinant of what we do with our life, and impacts all in our circle of influence. And as we bless, serve and reach out to others, our desire should be that they will be captivated by the same cause; that they will believe in and follow Jesus and become part of his movement to change the world.

Become

Our ultimate desire for those who are touched by the Kingdom should be that they become all that God designed them to be. Through a relationship with Jesus, and the transformative power of the Holy Spirit, they will take up their unique role in God's Kingdom and become more and more like Jesus every day.

I think one of the biggest challenges for those of us who have been part of the Church for some time is trusting God with the transformation of new believers. Our tendency is to map out the development of novice followers of Jesus, projecting onto them what we think they should be, and setting agendas for their compliance with our understanding of the principles and expectations of the Kingdom. We are often frustrated by the seeming lack of progress in the new believer, and although we acknowledge the power of God to transform lives, we find it hard to look past the glaring anomalies in behavior and lifestyle that we feel need to be addressed.

It is easy in this context to get ahead of God and start to meddle in the development of a new believer, missing what God is already doing in their life, and overriding his agenda for their spiritual development. We see behaviors we don't like and we try to change them before God is ready to deal with them.

What we often overlook is that behaviors are generated from the heart. The Bible tells us that out of the heart come all kinds of bad behavior.[87] But only God can change the state of the heart; so when we try to address behaviors alone, we are only treating symptoms and not the cause. Symptomatic treatment of a heart condition will never bring about permanent healing and change. Tinkering with behaviors, rather than the deep heart issues that are at the core of the behaviors, can result in superficiality and stagnancy in spiritual growth. In fact, focusing on symptoms alone sets up people for serious heart failure.

Our calling is to love people, no matter what their behaviors, and share with them the principles and values of the Kingdom, and then leave it up to God to bring about heart and behavioral change. We are all imperfect people, but some people's imperfections show in more obvious ways than others. Are our church communities gracious enough to embrace all people no matter what their behaviors? Can we accept people as they are and be patient and trust God enough to wait on him to bring about transformation, no matter how long it takes?

Jesus was regularly challenged by his disciples for the way he dealt with people, especially those who were not yet part of his Kingdom movement. The perspective of his disciples was generally very different to that of Jesus when it came to the way he addressed, ministered to and challenged the wide variety of individuals he encountered in his earthly ministry. Jesus often reprimanded his disciples for trying to apply their agenda to him or to others, alluding to their limited understanding of his plans and priorities.

Jesus was unpredictable and unconventional in his approach to those he encountered, often focusing on issues in a person's life that didn't at first appear to be the main issue that needed to be addressed. However, in his interaction with individuals or groups, Jesus consistently honed in on the very thing that was the key to their transformation, exposing through seemingly superficial conversation the core of a person's worldview, and revealing to them the radical change that was necessary for them to follow him. For example, in the middle of a theological discussion with Nicodemus, Jesus told him he had to be "born again," completely taking Nicodemus by surprise and directing their conversation down a theological and conceptual pathway that was radically different than anything Nicodemus would have expected.[88] For the Samaritan woman at the well, it was an abrupt command, "Go call your husband"—a request seemingly unrelated to their conversation—that cut to the heart of this woman's needs.[89] And, when the Jewish authorities were about to kill a woman caught in adultery, Jesus bent down and started to write on the ground with his finger, then deflected the attention from the woman's sin to the sin of her accusers, released the woman from her condemnation and guilt, and laid the foundation for her to start a new life.[90]

If we truly believe in the transformational power of Jesus, then we should be able to confidently hand people over to his care and trust him to mold and change them into who he wants them to be, following his timeline and sanctifying agenda. As much as we would like to see certain behaviors modified, misconceptions addressed and knowledge imparted, Jesus knows the crucial issues that need to be addressed first, and these are often not obvious to us.

So what is our role in discipling others in the way of Jesus? I believe that the best we can do for fellow followers of Jesus—particularly new believers—is to nurture their relationship with Jesus, walking the journey with them rather than directing their spiritual development. Spending time with people in prayer, talking to them about Jesus and his work in our own life and in the world, sharing what we are learning from God's Word and studying Scripture with those we are called to disciple—these are the things that will bring people closer to Jesus and allow the Holy Spirit to speak into their lives and mold them into authentic representatives of him. We need to steer away from the temptation to recreate people in our own image and let God have free rein in their lives; to recreate others into what he has designed them to be—unique and authentic representatives of Jesus.

CHAPTER 4

When the Kingdom Comes . . .

ORPHANS, WIDOWS AND THE NEEDY WILL RECEIVE CARE

Religion that God our Father accepts as pure and faultless is this: to look after orphans and widows in their distress and to keep oneself from being polluted by the world. (James 1:27)

Ashoka[91] lived in a rural area of Bangladesh. Her family was very poor and Ashoka and her siblings never knew a day without hunger. However, Ashoka felt she was fortunate. Only three in five babies born in her village survived the first five years of life, and Ashoka was now in her early teens. Her mother and father were still alive, whereas many of Ashoka's friends had lost at least one parent. Ashoka had even managed to attend school for a couple of years and had learned the basics of reading and writing. She had hopes and aspirations for a better life, while many in her village had lost all hope and were just managing to survive. But then all of Ashoka's dreams came crashing down as over a period of a few months both her parents became ill and died.

Ashoka did her best to care for her siblings, but was unable to find enough food even to feed herself, let alone her brothers and sisters. Her older brother and sister decided that they would leave the village and try to find work in one of

the cities close by. Ashoka never heard from either of them
again. Her younger sister and brother slowly succumbed
to malnutrition and after several bouts of illness both died.
Ashoka decided that the only way she was going to survive
would be to leave her village and to seek work in Dhaka, the
capital city of Bangladesh.

Ashoka became one of the thousands of young people
who pour into Dhaka each week seeking a better life. She was
able to survive a few weeks by scavenging food. Each day she
sought work but was unsuccessful in securing a job, until one
day she met a man in the street who told her he would help
her. He gave her some money and for the first time in her life
Ashoka was able to buy enough food to completely sate her
hunger. The next day Ashoka went to the address the man
had given her, and from that day on her life became a living
nightmare; she was put to work as a prostitute.

After an indeterminate period of abuse, deprivation and
suffering, Ashoka became pregnant. She had seen what had
happened to other girls who had been forced to have horrific
abortions. She decided she had to escape, and one night she
was finally able to get away.

Ashoka moved to another part of the city and once again
resorted to scavenging and begging to survive. She delivered
her baby on her own and continued begging for food on a
main thoroughfare that many people traversed on their way
to and from work.

One evening Ashoka was seen lying in her usual location
with her breast exposed and her baby suckling from her
breast. Everyone who saw her took a wide berth around her,
disgusted at her exposing herself. The next day she was once
again seen suckling her baby in the same place. Many hurled

abuse at her as they passed, telling her to cover herself. On the third morning, a man walked over to her and kicked her, telling her to move on. But Ashoka couldn't "move on" because she was dead. The news of this tragic situation spread rapidly throughout the day and eventually someone shared the story with Tanay,[92] a young follower of Jesus.

Tragic stories such as Ashoka's are not uncommon in Bangladesh. There is so much poverty and suffering in Dhaka city that people have become immune to the need. But Tanay felt he could no longer ignore the need; he had to do something. He recruited one of his friends to help him and they went to find the girl. Amazingly the baby was still alive. They took the baby home with them and arranged for Ashoka's body to be treated with respect and dignity.

It was as though the lights went on for Tanay, his friend and a widening circle of followers of Jesus who heard about Ashoka and her baby. The many needs that they had previously been able to gloss over—as just part of life in their city—suddenly became glaringly obvious. Those who had been touched by this tragic story could no longer ignore the need. In the past they had simply dismissed the injustice and suffering around them as being too big and too hard to deal with, and not their responsibility. Now they were faced with the reality that they could make a difference.

They asked others to join them in prayer to seek God's guidance as to how they could best serve him in such an overwhelmingly needy and complex environment. Through prayer, research and consultation, this expanding group of young believers became increasingly aware that they were being called to care for orphans who lived on the streets of their city.

They knew that there were no simple solutions; the orphans of Dhaka needed long-term care. It was difficult to know how to begin. It took an incredible amount of perseverance, advocacy and determination. But they were driven by a vision and a very clear biblical mandate. After a long period of planning, fundraising, partnership recruitment and miraculous provision of property and furnishings, they were able to establish an orphanage that would provide long-term care—that would take in parentless and homeless children in their early years and love them, educate them and care for them until they were able to live independently. The goal was to care for these children through to the completion of a high school education.

Over a short period of time three orphanages were established, and many more were planned. Ashoka's baby—along with many other orphans—was embraced by the Kingdom of God, is now thriving and has a promising future ahead of her, full of love, grace and opportunity to realize all her God-given potential.

Compassion

Throughout the Old Testament compassion is identified as an attribute of God. The Psalmists declare that "our God is full of compassion"[93] and "has compassion on all he has made."[94] In the New Testament God the Father is described as the "Father of Compassion"[95] and the Gospels identify Jesus' compassion as the primary driving force behind his ministry to people in need.

> When he saw the crowds, he had compassion on
> them, because they were harassed and helpless,
> like sheep without a shepherd. (Matthew 9:36)

When Jesus landed and saw a large crowd, he had compassion on them and healed their sick. (Matthew 14:14)

Jesus called his disciples to him and said, "I have compassion for these people; they have already been with me three days and have nothing to eat. I do not want to send them away hungry, or they may collapse on the way." (Matthew 15:32)

Jesus had compassion on them and touched their eyes. Immediately they received their sight and followed him. (Matthew 20:34)

Filled with compassion, Jesus reached out his hand and touched the man. "I am willing," he said. "Be clean!" (Mark 1:41)

When Jesus landed and saw a large crowd, he had compassion on them, because they were like sheep without a shepherd. So he began teaching them many things. (Mark 6:34)

"I have compassion for these people; they have already been with me three days and have nothing to eat." (Mark 8:2)

As we get closer to Jesus we become more like him, and becoming more like Jesus means that we are infused with his compassion for those in need—the lost, the sick, the orphaned, the hungry, the thirsty—both physically and spiritually.

In Colossians 3:12 we are instructed, "Therefore, as God's

chosen people, holy and dearly loved, clothe yourselves with compassion, kindness, humility, gentleness and patience." Compassion should be a vital and life-changing attribute of followers of Jesus.

Joey, a young man I mentor, captured the essential nature of compassion in a letter he wrote to me from Ethiopia, where he leads a ministry that cares for and empowers street children.

> Compassion releases the power of God; it releases the Kingdom of God! Compassion can be very raw and straight from the heart. It comes about in a moment quickly, often without warning. Compassion is not necessarily our reaction to a need, but our response to the Holy Spirit and His impression upon our heart. When we allow ourselves to be "moved with compassion," and combine this with faith for compassion's act, we get to see the Kingdom of God revealed. Compassion has been far too underrated for far too long. When applied with such faith it releases a love that never fails. We may not always get to see the fruit of that love in the moment, or in our lifetime, but that love never, ever fails. Praise God for all His compassion!

Bob Pierce

In 1948 Bob Pierce, a young pastor who was serving in the leadership of Youth for Christ, travelled to China and South Korea to share the Gospel with young people. During this trip he had an opportunity to speak to a group of students at a school in China. He told all the children the gospel story and challenged them to become followers of Jesus. He also asked them to go home and tell their parents about Jesus.

The next day, Pierce came back to the school to say farewell to the children before travelling back to the United States. While he was there, he noticed one little girl, White Jade, was badly beaten. He asked the school master, Tena Hoelkeboer, what had happened to her. Tena told Pierce that White Jade had gone home and told her parents about Jesus, declaring that she wanted to follow him. Her father had become extremely angry, had beaten White Jade severely and thrown her out of the home.

Pierce was horrified. He knew that Tena was already providing food and lodging for a number of children, and so he asked her if she would be able to care for White Jade as well. Tena responded that she simply did not have enough food or money to take in another child. So Bob Pierce committed to covering the cost of food, lodging and education for the girl. He began sending five dollars a month to sponsor White Jade.

This experience triggered something in Bob Pierce. It awakened a deep compassion for the needy, and he found himself committing to sponsor more and more destitute children as he traveled the world preaching the gospel. Pierce was not a wealthy man and he soon reached the limit of his personal resources. But he wanted to do more, and so he started recruiting other sponsors. In 1950, Bob Pierce founded World Vision, which has now become one of the largest Christian aid agencies in the world, operating in one hundred countries with more than thirty thousand full-time staff.[96] Pierce also went on to found Samaritan's Purse, which has also grown into a significant aid organization responding to many needs in the world, particularly in areas where there have been catastrophic natural disasters. During in his lifetime—impelled by the compassion of Jesus—Pierce served and blessed hundreds of millions of people.

Bob Pierce discovered through his experience in China that there was much more to serving in God's Kingdom than telling people about Jesus. He realized that responding to people's needs was part of the gospel, that blessing, loving and serving people was an essential element of introducing people to Jesus. Not long after his trip to China, Pierce captured his compassion for the lost and needy in a profound statement that he wrote on the fly-leaf of his Bible: "Let my heart be broken by the things that break the heart of God." This became his life motto and compelled him to make a huge impact in the world for the Kingdom of God.

As my young friend Joey wrote, "Compassion is not necessarily our reaction to a need, but our response to the Holy Spirit and His impression upon our heart. When we allow ourselves to be 'moved with compassion,' and combine this with faith for compassion's act, we get to see the kingdom of God revealed." Trying to conjure up compassion from some hidden recess in our psyche is not a plausible proposition. Compassion comes from the heart, and it is generated by the transformational work of the Holy Spirit. This transformation comes by opening ourselves up to God's regenerative power through prayer and submission—volitionally giving up the rights of our life to God, asking him to change us from within, and being prepared to embrace the disruption and sacrifice that will be part of our compassionate response to the needs around us.

Serving Jesus by Serving Others

I don't believe that a compassionate response to those in need is an "optional extra" in God's Kingdom. Compassion is an attribute of Jesus—an essential part of who he is—and consequently it should be a part of who we are if we claim to be followers of Jesus. The compassion of Jesus should define us. This is poignantly pointed out by Jesus in Matthew 25.

> When the Son of Man comes in his glory, and all the angels with him, he will sit on his throne in heavenly glory. All the nations will be gathered before him, and he will separate the people one from another as a shepherd separates the sheep from the goats. He will put the sheep on his right and the goats on his left.

> Then the King will say to those on his right, "Come, you who are blessed by my Father; take your inheritance, the kingdom prepared for you since the creation of the world. For I was hungry and you gave me something to eat, I was thirsty and you gave me something to drink, I was a stranger and you invited me in, I needed clothes and you clothed me, I was sick and you looked after me, I was in prison and you came to visit me."

> Then the righteous will answer him, 'Lord, when did we see you hungry and feed you, or thirsty and give you something to drink? When did we see you a stranger and invite you in, or needing clothes and clothe you? When did we see you sick or in prison and go to visit you?"

> The King will reply, "I tell you the truth,
> whatever you did for one of the least of these
> brothers of mine, you did for me."
>
> Then he will say to those on his left, "Depart
> from me, you who are cursed, into the eternal fire
> prepared for the devil and his angels. For I was
> hungry and you gave me nothing to eat, I was
> thirsty and you gave me nothing to drink, I was
> a stranger and you did not invite me in, I needed
> clothes and you did not clothe me, I was sick and
> in prison and you did not look after me."
>
> They also will answer, "Lord, when did we see
> you hungry or thirsty or a stranger or needing
> clothes or sick or in prison, and did not help
> you?"
>
> He will reply, "I tell you the truth, whatever you
> did not do for one of the least of these, you did
> not do for me."
>
> Then they will go away to eternal punishment,
> but the righteous to eternal life.

The way we respond to the physical, emotional, social and spiritual needs of those around us is an expression of the authenticity of our relationship with Jesus. Just breezing through life focusing upon our own needs, while ignoring the needs of those around us, is not an option Jesus leaves open to us.

The practical implication of this truth is sobering, particularly in the context of the wealthy Church in the Western world that so often focuses solely on the comforts and wants of its members. The compassion of Jesus doesn't only need to transform individuals but whole church communities. And this transformation, this infusion of compassion at the local Christian community level, should result in the redirection of finances and resources from providing more comfort for church members to meeting desperate needs in the local and global community.

Prioritized giving to the poor and needy

The capacity of a Christian community to respond to the needs around it has much to do with priorities. It is not that local churches can't do more for orphans, widows, the hungry, homeless and poor in their community, it is that there are other "more important" things that take precedence.

The early church certainly seemed to have priorities driven by the compassion of Jesus. In Acts and the Epistles we have several accounts of people giving, but the purpose of the giving and the allocation of the funds were significantly different from what we see in most churches today. A high priority of offerings in the early church was to meet the needs of the poor, widows, orphans and needy. For example:

> All the believers were together and had
> everything in common. Selling their possessions
> and goods, they gave to anyone as he had need.
> (Acts 2:44–45)

> There were no needy persons among them. For
> from time to time those who owned lands or
> houses sold them, brought the money from the

sales and put it at the apostles' feet, and it was
distributed to anyone as he had need. (Acts
4:34–35)

I would expect that there are very few local churches
today that have "giving to the poor and needy" as the top
expenditure item in their budget. The allocation of resources
to the poor and needy is probably one of the first items
that would be dropped from the budget if the church had a
financial shortfall.

When Jesus encountered people whose priorities were
skewed, he generally offered a very radical response. A classic
example of this was Jesus' interaction with the rich young
ruler—a person who was genuinely seeking to know what was
involved in following Jesus. The wealth of this man, and his
seeming disregard of those in need around him, was getting
in the way of him serving God and following Jesus. Jesus very
directly targeted this man's self-focused priorities, stating,
"One thing you lack. Go, sell everything you have and give
to the poor, and you will have treasure in heaven. Then come,
follow me."[97]

The Bible not only consistently directs believers to address
the needs of the poor, the widows, the orphans, the homeless
and the alien, but to actually make this a priority when it
comes to the allocation of funds and resources at the disposal
of both individuals and church communities.

Of course local churches do need a place to meet; having
a location—a focal point in the community—is important.
Looking after those who are called to minister in a church
is also a responsibility that cannot be overlooked. Resources
are needed to run a church. But the allocation of resources

must be in alignment with the priorities and mandates of the Kingdom of God.

Responding to the Needs

When I was starting out in my role as a pastor, I was at a loss as to where to begin. But by God's grace I stumbled onto a strategy that opened the door for the church to significantly impact the surrounding neighborhood for the Kingdom.

I wanted to know how we could best reach the people living in our neighborhood. So I started visiting the homes of people in our community, not the church members, but those who didn't come to our church. At nearly every home I visited I would be invited in and offered a "cuppa" (a cup of hot tea). As we sat and chatted over our tea I would say, "I believe our church exists to serve those who live in the local community, so what can we as a church do to serve you?" A simple question, but it generated some amazing conversations. I was astounded by how quickly people opened up and told of their deepest needs. The perspective and insight I gleaned from these home visits provided a blueprint for the church to build ministry that was the most appropriate to our local community needs.

We found that some of the greatest concerns and needs of the families in our area were associated with their teenage children. So we invested many of the church's resources in youth outreach and service programs. I started visiting the local high school and running activities for the students and seminars for parents. We initiated some innovative youth programs, including the live band coffee shop that I mentioned in the introduction to this book. We developed a youth counseling service and eventually hired a part-time youth worker who was a former local gang leader who had come to Jesus through our youth outreach ministries.

The church became inundated with young people, many of whom were unchurched and came with significant challenges and problems. It changed the church dramatically as it became populated by many "first generation" followers of Jesus. Parents, seeing the way the church responded to their needs and the positive impact this had on their teenage children, started attending the church. Many gave their lives to Jesus as well. It impacted the local community to such a degree that we ended up with people coming from other churches to see what it was that we were doing to reach the seemingly "unreachable."

During my home visits, another segment of our local community that I discovered had significant felt needs was young mothers. Many expressed their need for support, companionship and community. They felt isolated and alone in the challenging task of caring for their infants and toddlers. So we started a "Playgroup" program that targeted mothers with newborns through preschool children. Once again, because we were responding to a felt need in the local community, the program took off. As time passed we had to establish a second and third playgroup to accommodate all of the young mothers who wanted to participate.

Reallocating Resources

In Matthew's gospel, when Jesus is describing the Kingdom of God, he uses the example of a mustard seed. He explains, "The kingdom of heaven is like a mustard seed, which a man took and planted in his field. Though it is the smallest of all your seeds, yet when it grows, it is the largest of garden plants and becomes a tree, so that the birds of the air come and perch in its branches."[98]

Let me return briefly to the story of Julie that I told in the introduction. My somewhat reluctant compassionate response to Julie was a catalyst for a much more comprehensive response by the whole church community to homeless young people.

Julie was our mustard seed. The little seed of the Kingdom that was released in my life when I brought Julie to our home and cared for her began to grow. I started to become more aware of the needs of youth living in the neighborhood around the church. Julie introduced me to some of her friends and acquaintances. A number of them had similar challenges to Julie and were struggling with issues of homelessness, neglect and abuse. The seed sown by Julie started to grow, but the Lord had some more plowing and ground preparation to do in the church before the seed could take root and flourish.

Around the time that I met Julie, the church was growing rapidly and we had some significant challenges with parking. Every Sunday the small church parking lot filled up quickly, and many people had to park their cars on the street. Neighbors started to complain and so did the members of the church.

At a church leadership meeting it was decided that we would have to do something about the parking issue, and it seemed that the best solution would be to buy the house next door to the church and use the land as a parking lot. The problem with this plan was that the person who owned the house did not like the church one bit. Our neighbor, Jim,[99] had caused all kinds of problems, making official complaints to the local city authorities, calling the police when the youth were hanging out around the church and yelling abuse at church members who parked too close to his driveway. Nearly every Sunday morning, at the very time the sermon was being delivered, Jim would start his incredibly loud lawn mower and mow the grass right next to the fence line of the church, making it difficult to hear the message.

Since I was the pastor of the church, I was given the job of approaching Jim to ask him to sell us his house. I had already had a number of difficult conversations with Jim and had been told in very colorful language what he thought of me and the church. So I was not looking forward to my conversation about the possibility of buying his house. I asked the leaders of the church to pray, I spent much time in prayer, and I delayed the conversation as long as I could. Finally, on a Sunday afternoon, one day before the next church leadership meeting at which I was meant to report my progress with the house purchase, I drove up to the church determined to have a conversation with Jim about buying his home.

As I drove into the church parking lot I noticed Jim was working in his garden. As I got out of my car he came over to me, and before I could ask him anything, he said, "David, I want to talk to you about selling my house to the church." I was speechless. He went on to offer to sell his house to us for 10 percent less than the market value.

I couldn't wait for the leadership meeting. With much joy I reported the miraculous intervention of God and his amazing provision. We very quickly raised the funds for a deposit and secured a low interest loan to purchase the property. The purchase went through very smoothly and we immediately started making plans to demolish the house and construct the parking lot.

During the time that the house was purchased and plans were being developed for the parking lot, the youth ministry of the church was growing rapidly. It was getting more and more difficult to respond to all the opportunities opening up for us to reach young people.

As I investigated the needs of youth in our community, I discovered that the place where most of the marginalized and "at-risk" young people hung out was around the train station in our local shopping precinct. With some visionary input from the youth in the church, we decided that we should develop an outreach program in the shopping precinct. We obtained a double-decker bus, which had been imported from London, and set it up as a mobile coffee shop complete with tables and chairs and an industrial coffee machine.

Of course, we didn't have much trouble attracting youth. A brightly colored London double-decker bus really stood out in the parking lot! After a couple of weeks we actually had young people travelling on the train from different areas to visit the bus. One night, when we had packed up and were just about to leave, I noticed a bunch of young people still hanging out around the bus. It was the early hours of the morning, and I was a little concerned as to why these young people hadn't gone home. While I was chatting to them they asked if I could give them a ride to the local sports ground. When I inquired why they wanted to go to the sports ground, they told me they slept in the scoreboard. There were fourteen teenagers in the group, and all of them were homeless. The scoreboard provided a warm and protected place for them to sleep.

I ended up taking them to the sports ground because I didn't know what else to do. But I couldn't ignore their plight. These young people were incredibly vulnerable and desperately in need of shelter, care, love and protection. One of the girls had recently been raped by an unknown assailant.

Most of them were using drugs. Only a few of them were regularly attending school.

As I thought and prayed about these homeless young people through the week, the Holy Spirit convicted me and challenged me with a message I initially tried to ignore. But by the end of the week it was abundantly clear what Jesus wanted me to do. The message was loud and clear, "I didn't give you that house next door to the church so that you could knock it down and build a parking lot. I gave you the house so that you could use it to care for homeless youth."

It wasn't easy to deliver this message to the church leadership. I was unsure what their reaction would be, and was actually surprised at how well they received what I had to share with them. They said they would pray about it and would discuss the option of using the house for homeless young people at the next meeting. By the time the next meeting came around the Holy Spirit had done his work. All of the members of the leadership team were convinced that we should shelve our plans to build a parking lot and use the house to accommodate homeless young people.

We still had our parking problem, but by the grace of God we were able to put our comfort and convenience aside in the face of a far greater need. Our priorities were rearranged by Jesus, and great blessing resulted. The whole church community got behind the homeless young people program. They provided furnishings for the home and many meals each week. People in the church became the parents and grandparents that the young people lacked in their lives. The church community loved many of these young people into the Kingdom.

Of course, we very quickly ran out of room for the young

people who had need of accommodation. One night I met a girl named Helen whom I offered to drive home when our youth program had finished. She told me she couldn't go home, that she had a very violent boyfriend who had thrown her out of the place where they lived and had threatened to kill her if she came back. Our accommodation home was full. Jenny and I didn't have any room in our home for another young person.

Faced with the dilemma of having a very vulnerable young girl who desperately needed a place to say and someone to care for her, I came up with what seemed to me to be an obvious solution. My solution reflected my youthful naivety and the fact that I didn't really know the unspoken boundaries that often exist in a church community.

I put Helen in my car and drove to the home of one of the church families. I knew this couple had some spare bedrooms in their home, since two of their children had recently moved out. So with Helen in tow I knocked on their door. When the couple opened the door I introduced Helen, told them her story, and asked if they would look after her until I could find a more long-term solution. What could this couple say? They took Helen in.

Helen spent several weeks with this church family until I found a more permanent accommodation solution for her. She became part of our church community, and after experiencing the love and blessing of Jesus through many in the church, she too decided to follow him.

The homeless youth accommodation program continued to grow. I approached other churches in the area and encouraged them to set up accommodation homes as well. The program eventually grew to eighteen homes attached to various church communities along with thirty to forty families who were prepared to care for homeless young people on a regular basis. The church parking lot was never constructed.

The Church is not called to be self-serving, to focus all its attention on the needs and aspirations of its members. A self-serving local church community is an anathema to our God.[100] The Church has a wonderful capacity to meet the needs of people, but if we don't look outward and find out what these needs are, we will never be able to respond to them.

The most valuable resource of the Church is its people and their collective potential to bless others. As followers of Jesus it is our time, homes, cars, possessions, and above all, our capacity to love and care for others that God directs us to invest in meeting the needs of the poor, the lonely, the lost, the widows, the orphans, the homeless, the marginalized and alienated.

CHAPTER 5

When the Kingdom Comes . . .

JUSTICE WILL PREVAIL

Stop doing wrong, learn to do right! Seek justice, encourage the oppressed. Defend the cause of the fatherless, plead the case of the widow. (Isaiah 1:16–17)

Jenny and my first mission experience was serving in an Aboriginal community on the edge of the desert in Western Australia caring for abused and neglected Aboriginal children. When God called us we were in our early twenties, recently married and both had very promising careers. But God made it abundantly clear that he wanted us to give up our own aspirations and dreams and follow his agenda for our lives.

After wrestling with this call for many months, we finally yielded and asked God what it was he wanted us to do. His reply was that he wanted us to serve the most marginalized and vulnerable people in our nation—abandoned, abused and orphaned Aboriginal children. We resigned from our jobs, sold the land we had purchased to build our dream home, gathered together our few possessions and moved to Western Australia.

It wasn't long after we arrived at the Aboriginal community that we had a number of children placed in our care. Our hearts were broken as we were confronted with the injustice and abuse that these children had experienced. Often children were sent to us in a terrible state—malnourished, suffering chronic diarrhea and infested with scabies and lice. We would take them in and provide them with clothing, nourishing food and medical care and love them with the love of Jesus.

We were surprised and deeply affected by the suffering and deprivation we encountered in a wealthy and developed nation such as Australia. God gave us a special love for these children and our hearts overflowed with his compassion as we took one child after another into our care. But the thing that caught us by surprise, the thing that we didn't anticipate, the thing that generated an overwhelming sense of outrage, was the gross injustice experienced by some of the Aboriginal children and adults at the hands of people who were in positions of power and entrusted to provide care and services to these people.

Abandoned and abused Aboriginal children are often made "wards of the state." In essence the government becomes their parent and is responsible for placing these children with families. People who take the children in are paid by the government to do so, and thus there is significant incentive for families to foster Aboriginal children.

It was in this foster care system that we encountered some examples of terrible injustice and abuse. In some cases, the only reason families took these children into their homes was so that they could receive the government payment. In these situations the children were often treated poorly—ignored and neglected, excluded from family activities, and certainly not loved as a child should be loved. In extreme cases the children were beaten and abused.

It appalled us that the very people being commissioned

and paid to care for Aboriginal children were subjecting them to abuse. We met with government workers to advocate for better treatment of these children and did all we could to fight this injustice. But the problems were deeply systemic and complex and we largely felt powerless to change the systems that allowed the injustices to continue.

As Jenny and I came across more and more examples of injustice we realized our experiences were awakening in us something new. We were progressively developing a deeper sense of God's call to address the injustices we encounter in the world. With this heightened awareness of our Kingdom responsibility to fight injustice, we found ourselves in a position where we could do something that would make a difference.

One of our tasks was to manage the store that provided food and household goods for the people living in the community. We started noticing that a number of the Aboriginal adults who received pensions from the government (social security payments) ran out of money a few days after they received their pension payment. For the remainder of the two weeks before their next payment they were unable to even buy food for their families. We gave them food or provided credit so they could buy goods from the store.

After questioning local community members and observing how they handled money, we discovered what was happening. The Aboriginal people would go into the local town of Kalgoorlie to pick up their pension check, and then they would go to a bank or store to exchange it for cash. Many of the older Aboriginal people had little sense of the value of money and people were taking advantage of them. At the bank the clerk would often cash their check but only give them a portion of the value of the check and pocket the rest of the money. At the stores in the town, the Aboriginal people would hand over all of their cash to pay for a low cost item, but would only get a small amount of change in return.

I was incensed by this gross injustice. I asked a friend who served in the local police force whether he could do anything about it. He told me that there was really nothing he could do. He would need to catch the bank clerks and shop keepers in the act of cheating the Aboriginal people before he could prosecute anyone, and there were many other policing issues with a much higher priority. He explained that this practice of defrauding Aboriginal people was so pervasive that it was almost impossible to wipe out.

But we weren't going to give up so easily. We went to our bank and asked them if they would allow us to cash pension checks in our store and then bank them into our account. The bank agreed to do this for us. We told the people in our community that we would cash their checks. A few tried us out, and when they received a lot more cash than they had been receiving previously, they told other community members. They also started buying all their food and goods from our store, because they realized they were able to buy much more with their money than in the stores in town.

What we didn't realize was how much impact our simple response to an injustice was going to have on the broader Aboriginal community in the area. The people in our community started spreading the word. It wasn't long before Aboriginal people who lived in Kalgoorlie started making a forty kilometer[101] round trip to our community just to cash their checks.

The practice of cheating Aboriginal people out of their

pension checks was not stopped by our actions, but the injustice was addressed, and the Aboriginal people now had an option available where they knew they would be treated honestly and fairly.

The Aboriginal people had been touched by the Kingdom of God, and their experience of the Kingdom was one of justice, kindness and goodness.

Advocates for Justice

What is the role of the Church in society? It is to be a light to the nations, shining the light of God's grace, goodness, honesty and truth to others who have yet to experience the salvation and blessings of the Kingdom.[102] It is to go out into the world with a comprehensive gospel, a gospel that advocates for Jesus and is characterized by the fruit of the Spirit,[103] justice, truth, grace and service to others.

There is much injustice in this world. It is all around us. How are we responding as followers of Jesus or as members of a local church community? Are we even aware of the injustices around us? Are we interested at all in doing something about injustice?

If we are not aware of injustice, or if we choose to ignore it, then we won't have to do anything about it. Taking on injustice is never easy. It is often deeply systemic and perpetrated by powerful people. But God doesn't give us the option of ignoring injustice.

In Isaiah 1:17 we are told, "Learn to do right! Seek justice, encourage the oppressed. Defend the cause of the fatherless, plead the cause of the widow." And in Isaiah 58:6, "Is not this the kind of fasting I have chosen: to loose the chains of injustice and untie the cords of the yoke, to set the oppressed free and break every yoke?" Proverbs 31:8–9 instructs us to "Speak up for those who cannot speak for themselves, for the rights of all who are destitute. Speak up and judge fairly; defend the rights of the poor and needy." And Proverbs 29:7 declares, "The righteous care about justice for the poor, but the wicked have no such concern." God clearly directs us in his Word to address injustice.

In developed nations injustice is often more hidden than in poorer developing nations and it is easier to ignore, but we don't have to look far to find it. Injustice is nearly always associated with someone in a position of power or influence oppressing, manipulating, taking advantage of or simply ignoring vulnerable and needy people. It is a pervasive malady in the broader society, but it is also evident in the Church.

One of the most horrific examples of injustice and oppression in the United States is the juvenile sex trade. The US Department of Justice estimates that more than 250,000 American youth are at risk of becoming victims of commercial sexual exploitation. Vulnerable children and youth between ages twelve and fourteen are prime targets for organized crime units, with many of the children sold into the sex trade coming from broken families or the foster care system.[104] In addition to domestic girls who are exploited, about 45,000 to 50,000 girls from other countries are smuggled into the United States and enslaved by organized sex trade cartels each year.[105]

The trafficking and enslavement of young people is a blight on society and should not be ignored by followers of Jesus. The Church needs to invest in solutions, partner with those trying to rescue enslaved young people and expose and tear down the systemic structures that allow this horrific practice to thrive and grow.

Many organizations and ministries endeavor to address injustice—including human trafficking—both domestically and globally. Investing in and partnering with these organizations and ministries is one way to get involved. Making ourselves aware through research and investigation is also another pathway to involvement. As followers of Jesus become aware of the injustice in the world around them, the Holy Spirit is able to direct and mobilize the believer to respond. Proactive investigation of Kingdom advancing opportunities provides knowledge for the Holy Spirit to work with, whereas ignorance and inaction quell the Holy Spirit and are often the protective mechanisms we employ to avoid Kingdom imperatives disrupting our lives.

A wonderful example of a follower of Jesus making a huge difference in the world by addressing a glaring injustice is that of William Wilberforce's advocacy for the abolition of slavery—a story that was so well portrayed in the widely acclaimed film *Amazing Grace*. Wilberforce could have easily ignored the issue of slavery and moved on with his very promising political career. But he was so compelled by his devotion to Jesus and the mandates of God's Word to address injustice that he was prepared to embrace rejection, ridicule, attacks on his character and alienation to pursue the abolition of the brutal slave trade.

Wilberforce's perseverance was astonishing. He headed the parliamentary campaign against the British slave trade for twenty-six years until the passage of the Slave Trade Act in 1807. Even after resigning from Parliament in 1826 because of his failing health, Wilberforce continued his involvement, supporting the campaign for the complete abolition of slavery. That campaign led to the Slavery Abolition Act of

1833, which abolished slavery in most of the British Empire. Wilberforce died just three days after hearing that the Act was going to be passed by the British Parliament.

Wilberforce was an advocate for those who had no voice. The victims of slavery were powerless to fight the oppressive, brutal and dehumanizing treatment they were being subjected to. They needed someone who had influence and the capacity to represent them in their fight for justice and freedom. This is the role that Jesus is calling us to—to be advocates for the oppressed and fight for the victims of injustice. We should use whatever influence, power and resources we have at our disposal to redress acts of repression, enslavement, victimization and unjust treatment of others.

Fighting the global injustices such as slavery and human trafficking is a Kingdom responsibility, but we should not limit ourselves to global issues. We need to pay special attention to our own community, to where we live and work, to our immediate circle of influence. We do not have to look far to find examples of injustice all around us.

As we come across injustice in our local communities, although we may not be able to completely dismantle the systems that support injustice, we should strive to provide an avenue for people to escape the unjust behavior of others. In the example of our response to the defrauding of Aboriginal people in Kalgoorlie, although we were somewhat powerless to address the larger problem, we were able to provide a way out for those being unjustly treated in our local area. Providing options for escape is a worthy Kingdom response to those who are entrapped in systems of abuse and injustice.

Acting Justly

In addition to directing us to address the injustices of the world around us, the Bible also has strongly worded imperatives that demand that we pay special attention to the injustices within the Church itself. In fact, God reserves some of his most scathing and confrontational condemnations for those who claim to be his followers and yet perpetrate injustice or allow unjust behavior to continue within communities of faith.

In Isaiah 1 God told the people of Israel what he thought of their "church" activities and services in the context of the injustice that they were not only practicing, but also overlooking in their communities:

"The multitude of your sacrifices—
what are they to me?" says the LORD.
"I have more than enough of burnt offerings,
of rams and the fat of fattened animals;
I have no pleasure
in the blood of bulls and lambs and goats.
When you come to appear before me,
who has asked this of you,
this trampling of my courts?
Stop bringing meaningless offerings!
Your incense is detestable to me.
New Moons, Sabbaths and convocations—
I cannot bear your evil assemblies.
Your New Moon festivals and your appointed feasts
my soul hates.
They have become a burden to me;
I am weary of bearing them.

When you spread out your hands in prayer,
I will hide my eyes from you;
even if you offer many prayers,
I will not listen.
Your hands are full of blood;
wash and make yourselves clean.
Take your evil deeds
out of my sight!
Stop doing wrong,
learn to do right!
Seek justice,
encourage the oppressed.
Defend the cause of the fatherless,
plead the case of the widow."[106]

Amos also identifies injustice as something that God cannot tolerate in his people:

For three sins of Israel, even for four, I will
not turn back my wrath. . . . They trample on
the heads of the poor as upon the dust of the
ground and deny justice to the oppressed. . . .
Now then, I will crush you as a cart crushes
when loaded with grain.[107]

In his condemnation of the Pharisees and Jewish religious leaders Jesus identified injustice as one of the primary disqualifiers to them being in any way representative of or aligned with God and his Kingdom.

Woe to you Pharisees, because you give God a
tenth of your mint, rue and all other kinds of

garden herbs, but you neglect justice and the
love of God. You should have practiced the
latter without leaving the former undone.[108]

The recent pedophilia scandal in the Catholic Church
has discredited the Kingdom of God globally, bringing
dishonor to God and his people. What has attracted universal
condemnation across the world is not only the deviant and
predatory behavior of priests within the church, but the fact
that the church leadership allowed this to go on for years,
ignoring the problem even in the face of overwhelming
evidence that young people were being sexually molested.

And this systemic institutionalized pedophilia extends
well beyond the confines of the Catholic Church. Several
mission and Protestant church boarding schools are now
uncovering and reporting cases of sexual molestation of
students by school staff. Once again this was over extended
periods of time with no action taken by leadership.[109]

The predatory sexual behavior of pastoral leaders in the
Church is another example of injustice being perpetrated
by those who claim to represent Jesus. There are constant
revelations in the media of prominent pastors having sexual
affairs with church staff or congregational members. Many of
the victims of this predatory behavior have been vulnerable
people who have sought counseling or support from the pastor
and have been manipulated or lured into a sexual relationship.
Instead of using their influence and pastoral gifts to bless and
serve others, the offenders have used their position of trust to
prey on the vulnerable.

Injustice in the church takes many forms other than sexual
abuse and predatory behavior. Injustice occurs when a church

has the wealth and resources to care for the needy in their congregation and yet neglects to meet their needs. Injustice occurs when funds faithfully given by followers of Jesus to advance his Kingdom and to serve others are inappropriately used to enrich the church leadership or to prop up or increase the wealth of institutional structures. Injustice occurs when some members of a church community are repressed, treated with disrespect or disdain, or, inversely, when other members of a church community are treated with favor.[110]

If we are followers of Jesus our commission is to seek out injustice within and outside of our communities of faith and get involved in fighting it. Deliberately pursuing injustice is a responsibility of any member of God's Kingdom. Seeking God's guidance and enlightenment is a great starting point for getting involved. Our prayer should be: "Lord, please show me where I am being unjust in my dealings with others. Show me in my church and my community and the world where injustice is occurring, and guide and direct me in my response to these injustices. Empower me to be an effective advocate for those who have no voice, who are oppressed and victimized, and who need to experience your love, grace and justice."

When those who are victims of injustice encounter God's Kingdom they should experience solidarity and support— they should find someone who cares about their plight and is willing to join them in their struggle.

"Let justice roll on like a river, righteousness like a never-failing stream!"[111]

CHAPTER 6

When the Kingdom Comes . . .

PEOPLE WILL BE HEALED

*As you go, preach this message: "The kingdom of heaven is near."
Heal the sick, raise the dead, cleanse those who have leprosy, drive out
demons. Freely you have received, freely give. (Matthew 10:7–8)*

Isabella[112] was in pain again. The pain came in waves that doubled her over in agony. It was most intense in her stomach, but extended into her back and shoulders. Her husband, Alejandro,[113] was at a loss as to what he could do for her. Over several months Isabella's pain had been progressively getting worse, and now the over-the-counter pain killers no longer seemed to be making a difference. But they couldn't afford the $120 it would cost to visit a doctor, let alone the enormous costs associated with the tests and consultations that would surely result from further investigation.

Alejandro's laboring job didn't provide medical insurance.[114] In fact, the company he worked for was struggling to even pay salaries, let alone cover the ever-increasing medical insurance costs of their employees. Their financial situation was grim and they barely had enough to pay their rent and feed themselves and their children.

Isabella was in so much pain this time that Alejandro considered taking her to the emergency department of the local hospital. But friends had taken their sick child to the hospital emergency department recently and had received a bill for $22,000. They were able to negotiate a discount with the hospital, along with a payment plan, but they now owed the hospital $15,000 and the payments were crippling them financially.

Alejandro didn't want to leave Isabella alone, but he had to go to work. He made her as comfortable as he could and in tears drove to the location of his company's latest building project. When he walked onto the building site Mike, one of the carpenters working on the project, couldn't help but notice that something was wrong. He asked Alejandro what was going on, and when Alejandro told him about Isabella's illness, Mike said he had an idea of where Alejandro may be able to get some help.

Mike had heard about a church that recently started providing free medical services for people like Alejandro and Isabella. The church had secured access to an old motor home that had been converted into a medical clinic. Twice a month they parked the vehicle at a local shopping center and offered free medical consultation and services to families and individuals who didn't have medical insurance. It just happened to be the first Wednesday of the month and that was one of the nights when the medical clinic was available.

After work, Alejandro rushed home, asked his neighbors to look after the children, got Isabella into the car, and drove her to the location where the church provided the medical service. It wasn't long before a big motor home pulled into the parking lot, followed by a volunteer doctor as well as other support staff.

Isabella was not very confident speaking English, but Alejandro soon discovered that one of the volunteers and the nurse were both fluent in Spanish. The volunteer reception staff took down Isabella's details and it wasn't long before the doctor saw her. After a thorough examination the doctor realized that Isabella's condition was serious and told her that he was going to refer her to a gastroenterologist.

Isabella was horrified; she could not afford to see a specialist. The doctor explained that they had a network of specialists who were prepared to offer their services free to people referred to them from the Mobile Clinic. He gave her some prescription pain medication to relieve her symptoms until she was able to see the specialist.

Alejandro and Isabella left the clinic that night with hope. They knew they had a challenging road ahead but were assured that Isabella could be effectively treated for her condition. Eventually Isabella was able to see the specialist and receive the care she required. Alejandro and Isabella's encounter with the Kingdom of God had brought them healing and health.

The church that provides this mobile medical clinic is a small church community that meets in an outlet mall in a city on the outskirts of Denver, Colorado. They don't have a lot of resources and, as is the case with many smaller churches, struggle to cover their church budget. But as the leadership of the church became increasingly aware of the needs of people living in their surrounding neighborhoods, they responded by allocating more of their resources to serving their local community. One of the most glaring needs was access to basic medical services for people like Alejandro and Isabella.

The church leadership realized that within their

congregation, and other congregations in their city, they had access to many medical professionals. It was obvious what the church's Kingdom responsibilities required of them. It was simply a matter of connecting the resource with the need.

Jesus Heals

As Jesus walked this earth he constantly encountered people who needed physical, emotional and spiritual healing. He ministered to these people at their point of need, often miraculously healing a physical condition or illness as well as dealing with deeper spiritual and emotional issues.

When the gospel writers record Jesus' healings they regularly associate the healing with the coming of the Kingdom of God:

> Jesus went throughout Galilee, teaching in their synagogues, preaching the good news of the kingdom, and healing every disease and sickness among the people. (Matthew 4:23)

> Jesus went through all the towns and villages, teaching in their synagogues, preaching the good news of the kingdom and healing every disease and sickness. (Matthew 9:35)

> And the people all tried to touch him, because power was coming from him and healing them all. Looking at his disciples, he said: "Blessed are you who are poor, for yours is the kingdom of God." (Luke 6:19–20)

But the crowds learned about it and followed
him. He welcomed them and spoke to them
about the kingdom of God, and healed those
who needed healing. (Luke 9:11)

Jesus specifically mentions healing when he commissions
his followers to take the Kingdom message to others:

As you go, preach this message: "The kingdom
of heaven is near." Heal the sick, raise the
dead, cleanse those who have leprosy, drive out
demons. Freely you have received, freely give.
(Matthew 10:7–8)

And he sent them out to preach the kingdom of
God and to heal the sick. (Luke 9:2)

After this the Lord appointed seventy-two
others and sent them two by two ahead of him
to every town and place where he was about
to go. . . . "Heal the sick who are there and tell
them, 'The kingdom of God is near you.'" (Luke
10:1, 9)

Healing is intrinsic to the ministry of Jesus and the
coming of the Kingdom. As authentic representatives of Jesus
bringing the Kingdom of God to the world, healing should
be a component of what we bring.

Medical Healing

There are many ways that we can provide healing for people. As in the case of Alejandro and Isabella, providing access to medical services is one of those ways. Most churches have medical professionals in their congregations that can be mobilized to provide healing services to people in their congregations and neighboring communities.

Of course, another way to help people access medical services is to provide the funds they require to get the care they need. I know of a number of churches and individual followers of Jesus who have provided the funds to pay medical bills for people who cannot afford medical care. Others liaise with local doctors and medical clinics to provide medical services to impoverished people at no cost, or for a significantly discounted fee.

One of the most well-known parables of Jesus is the story of "The Good Samaritan."[115] It poignantly defines the response of true citizens of the Kingdom toward those they encounter who are in need of care and healing. Not only did the Samaritan provide immediate medical care, he also paid for ongoing services.

This story contrasts a religious response with a Kingdom response to someone needing care and healing. The two religious leaders who passed by the man and ignored his need were representative of the institutional church leadership at the time of Jesus. As people who professed to serve God and his Kingdom, the priest and Levite were the most likely candidates to provide for this man in his distress and suffering; but in the end it was a despised and hated Samaritan who exhibited a godly response.

As well as explaining what authentic Kingdom care looks like, Jesus also used this parable to alert us to the dangers of "religiosity," of how far from the Kingdom we can stray when we focus on religious practice rather than our relationship with Jesus and his principles of living and community. Samaritans were considered by the established religious community of the time to be theologically and spiritually awry. The fact that it was a Samaritan whom Jesus commended for being the most authentic representative of God was a sobering lesson for all present, especially the religious leaders.

In the circle of influence of any follower of Jesus are "neighbors" who need healing. Are we going to respond as the religious leaders did in the story of the Good Samaritan, ignoring the need; or are we going to be true Kingdom neighbors ministering to the medical needs of those around us, providing ongoing care and healing?

One of the condemnations God leveled at the religious leaders of Israel was their self-centeredness, primarily expressed in lack of practical response to the sick and injured. In Ezekiel 34 we read, "This is what the Sovereign Lord says: Woe to the shepherds of Israel who only take care of themselves! Should not shepherds take care of the flock? You eat the curds, clothe yourselves with the wool and slaughter the choice animals, but you do not take care of the flock. You have not strengthened the weak or healed the sick or bound up the injured."[116]

Global Healing

The commands and directives in God's Word for us to minister to those who are sick extend beyond our immediate neighborhood to the whole of humanity. When considering disease and illness, what would it look like for the Kingdom to come globally?

There is great disparity in access to health care in the world. Around 20 percent of the world's population resides in the wealthiest and most developed countries, yet they use 90 percent of the funds spent on health care globally.[117] Almost ten million children under the age of five die every year from preventable diseases and medical conditions.[118]

Providing adequate medical care for all humanity is a complex and overwhelming dilemma. But it is something that followers of Jesus should not ignore. There are many ways to get involved, either directly or in partnership with others who are strategically placed and equipped to make a difference. I believe that part of the mosaic of Kingdom activity of every local church should be some involvement in meeting the medical and health needs of those living in the poorest and least resourced areas of the world.

Miraculous Healing

There are few biblical instructions given to followers of Jesus about the practice or process of miraculous healing. In the Gospels, Acts and the Epistles we read accounts of the disciples and Paul healing people in the name and power of Jesus.[119] In 1 Corinthians the gift of healing is mentioned, although we are not told how this gift is to be used.[120]

In James 5 we get the clearest instructions to the church about the process to be followed in seeking the Lord's intervention when someone is sick: "Is any one of you sick? He should call the elders of the church to pray over him and anoint him with oil in the name of the Lord. And the prayer offered in faith will make the sick person well; the Lord will raise him up."[121]

We are told in God's Word that "Jesus Christ is the same yesterday and today and forever."[122] Just as he healed when he was here on this earth—and authorized his disciples to heal[123]—so Jesus can and does heal today and he gives his followers the authority to heal.

I have served as both a pastor and an elder of a church and have on numerous occasions followed the directives of James 5 in ministering to sick and injured people. On a number of occasions I believe God miraculously intervened. In one case a woman in our church had terminal cancer and was told by her doctor that they could do no more for her and she only had a few months left to live. We anointed her with oil and prayed for her. It wasn't long after our time of prayer that she had further medical tests and the doctors reported that the cancer had ceased to spread. She eventually went into complete remission.

It seems to me that in response to prayer for healing we often see the healing occur in conjunction with the medical treatment being received, with God using medical resources and the skills of medical professionals to express his healing power. Jesus took the bread and fish offered by a little boy and miraculously multiplied these tangible offerings to feed thousands of people. Surely Jesus can take the "bread and fish" of our medical knowledge and resources and miraculously use them to heal people. I have heard doctors use the term "miraculous" several times in describing the response to medical treatment of a person we have prayed for.

Other times I have joined with others in anointing people

with oil and praying for their healing and they have not recovered from their illness. Is this due to our unrighteousness or lack of faith? I don't think it is. When sick people don't respond to our prayers, I think it has much more to do with God's sovereignty than it has to do with us.

Whenever someone was healed through the ministry of the disciples, they went to great lengths to explain that it was Jesus who healed and not them.[124] They continually acknowledged the sovereignty of God in the miracles that accompanied their ministry. When we ask God to heal someone we should do so believing that he has the power to miraculously heal, while also acknowledging that he has the right to say no to our request.

Anecdotally, it seems that there is less miraculous healing evident in wealthy nations that are well served by sophisticated medical services than in nations without the medical resources to treat the sick and injured. When the Bible instructs us to provide healing and care to the sick and injured it sometimes refers to miraculous healing and at other times refers to human medical care and intervention. Both, I believe, are valid responses to our injunction from God to provide healing.

Recently I was in Rwanda at a gathering of East African Youth for Christ leaders. We had a number of people from the United States with us participating in some of the events at this gathering. One of the participants was chatting with a leader from an impoverished East African nation. He asked her about medical care, specifically inquiring whether they had medical insurance to pay for medical services for her and her many staff and volunteers. She explained that medical insurance was not an option, and even if they did have some way to pay for medical services, for most of her people it was impossible to even access a doctor. In one area where they worked there were only four doctors serving hundreds of thousands of people. Shocked by her answer, this man asked what they did when they were sick or injured. Her reply was simple, "We pray for healing, of course!" It is in these environments with little or no access to medical care that I most often hear about miraculous healing and meet people who have been healed.

Emotional Healing

I would be remiss if I did not make mention of the desperate need for emotional healing in our world today. Emotional wounds are generally far more difficult to deal with than physical injuries and ailments. Many of the references in the Bible that address suffering and God's ministry to those who suffer allude to, or directly speak to, emotional pain. A good example of this is in Job, where Job shares, "And now my life ebbs away; days of suffering grip me. . . . The churning inside me never stops; days of suffering confront me.."[125] Later in Job Elihu reflects, "But those who suffer he delivers in their suffering; he speaks to them in their affliction."[126]

Throughout the book of Psalms David shares much of his personal anguish, heartache and emotional pain. Also in the Psalms we get glimpses of God ministering to David at the depth of his soul with the healing balm of his grace, love and goodness. Psalm 23 captures this healing of the emotions beautifully: "He restores my soul . . . for you are with me; your rod and your staff, they comfort me. . . . Surely goodness and love will follow me all the days of my life."[127]

When Elijah was deeply depressed after his confrontation
with Jezebel—so emotionally distraught that he wanted to
die[128]—God ministered to him in ways that brought healing
and restoration. First, God revealed his character to Elijah,
showing him his might and power, but blessing and healing
him with a gentleness that was profound, speaking to him
in a "gentle whisper."[129] Second, God assured Elijah that he
was not alone, that there were many others in fellowship with
him, prepared to die for what Elijah stood for, and willing to
stand with him against the oppressors of his nation.[130]

One of the most effective things we can do for people
who are in emotional pain is to let them know that they are
not alone. To let them know that someone cares and will
be there for them whenever needed; to journey with them
through their pain to the place of healing and "restoration of
their soul." When people have suffered a great loss there are
very few words that will bring comfort. Many well-meaning
people in these situations offer empty platitudes that often
generate greater pain or even anger rather than comfort. In
most cases little needs to be said; just being there is enough.

When Jesus was on this earth he didn't only heal physical
suffering; he also addressed the emotional pain of many he
ministered to. For the woman caught in adultery, he stood with
her against the condemnation and self-righteous indignation
of the religious leaders, releasing her from her guilt and shame,
telling her that she was no longer condemned and providing
hope and opportunity for restoration.[131] For the Samaritan
woman he met at the well, Jesus cut right through her
masks and protective façade, revealing her deepest need and
providing restoration and healing. Her encounter with Jesus
profoundly changed her life, so much so that her testimony
about what Jesus did for her impacted many in her town.[132]

The greatest need for the young people who came into our care through the homeless youth accommodation program mentioned in Chapter 4 was emotional healing. These young people were deeply emotionally wounded—victims of abuse, violence, abandonment, alienation, deprivation and betrayal by those who professed to care about them. Many were very hard to love, exhibiting obnoxious behavior including substance abuse, drunkenness, offensive language, violence and anger. But the church community—both young people and adults— embraced them with love and acceptance regardless of their behavior. They prayed for them and sometimes with them; they provided meals for them and invited them to their homes; they helped get them employment and advocated for them when they messed up; they helped them fix their cars, took them surfing, played music with them and invited them to birthday parties; in many practical ways they let them know that they were loved and gave them hope.

All of this care and love resulted in "miraculous" healing for many of these young people. They were transformed by their encounter with Jesus and his healing power extended to them through the community of his followers who cared for them. They completed their schooling, secured steady employment and successfully moved into independent living. Some went on to become pastors and ministry leaders; others became leaders in their chosen profession.

So miraculous was the emotional healing and transformation of these young people that not only other churches and Christian agencies came to see what we were doing, but government welfare agency leaders started taking notice. The government sent us some of their hardest cases— the young people in their care with the most problems—

and when these young people were healed and transformed by the power of Jesus, the government started funding the accommodation program. They bought houses for us to expand the program, they helped pay for staff, and they subsidized the domestic and educational costs of some of the young people in our care.

In the same way Jesus accepted and loved us, he calls us to love others, to accept them with all their pain and ugliness and to minister to them at their deepest level of need. Providing emotional support and healing is part of our Kingdom role, and loving people with the unconditional love of Jesus is the most effective way to "restore their souls."

CHAPTER 7

When the Kingdom Comes . . .

THERE WILL BE ADEQUATE FOOD AND WATER FOR ALL

Feed the hungry, and help those in trouble. Then your light will shine out from the darkness, and the darkness around you will be as bright as noon. (Isaiah 58:10 NLT)

Johnny[133] lived in a rural village in the East African nation of Burundi. The civil war had devastated his country and Johnny's father and mother were continually worried about their safety and, in particular, the safety of their son. Johnny was four years old when the rebels came to his village and started slaughtering people indiscriminately. As the rebels moved through the village toward Johnny's home, his father and mother hid him under some bushes, but before they too could find a hiding place the rebels caught them. From under the bushes Johnny watched as his mother and father were hacked to death with machetes.

When the rebels left, Johnny didn't know what to do and for a few days just sat by the bodies of his father and mother. The rebels had stripped the village and Johnny could find no food in his home or in the few houses around him. He was already malnourished for it was rare that his parents could provide more than one meager meal a day. Johnny's hunger became so intense that in desperation he resorted to eating parts of his father's decaying body. He eventually wandered away from his home and along with other orphans went from village to village begging for food and somehow managing to survive.

Desperate for food and so weak from hunger he could hardly stand, Johnny finally joined many others at a rubbish dump outside a city. He started digging in the dirt and mud, and when he found anything that looked like food he ate it, along with the mud and stones he had excavated. He lived on the rubbish dump for a year until he was found by some staff of Youth for Christ.

When Youth for Christ found Johnny he was in a terrible state. They had to cut out stones that had been forced into his gums as he ate the mud from the dump. Apart from the expected consequences of years of malnutrition, Johnny had not grown or developed physically since witnessing his parents' murder. The trauma he had experienced had somehow affected him physiologically. He was seven years old when he was found by Youth for Christ, but only had the stature of a three-year-old.

Youth for Christ placed Johnny in one of their orphanages. They fed him and clothed him and provided the love and care he desperately needed. But although he regained the health and functionality he had lost due to years of malnutrition, he didn't seem to be growing at all physically.

After some months, through his interaction with the other children and the Youth for Christ staff, Johnny learned about Jesus. He asked many questions and slowly gained a deeper understanding of who Jesus was and what he taught about love and forgiveness. Johnny decided he wanted to be a follower of Jesus, and one night he handed over his life to the person he had come to know through the staff and other children of the orphanage.

The love, grace and forgiveness of Jesus infused Johnny's life and a miracle happened. He started to grow—physically, emotionally and spiritually. Although still somewhat small, Johnny is now within the normal range of size for a boy his age.

Feed the Hungry

In Psalm 107:9 we are told that God "satisfies the thirsty and fills the hungry with good things." Psalm 146:7 tells us, "He upholds the cause of the oppressed and gives food to the hungry." Our God is concerned for the hungry and thirsty and expects us to be the same.

There are unequivocal injunctions in the Bible for God's people to feed the hungry:

> Is not this the kind of fasting I have chosen: . . .
> Is it not to share your food with the hungry and
> to provide the poor wanderer with shelter—
> when you see the naked, to clothe him, and not
> to turn away from your own flesh and blood?
> (Isaiah 58:6–7)

> A righteous man…gives his food to the hungry
> and provides clothing for the naked. (Ezekiel
> 18:5, 7)

If your enemy is hungry, give him food to eat; if he is thirsty, give him water to drink. (Proverbs 25:21)

Jesus was concerned for people who were hungry and fed them. When confronted with the hunger of the crowds that came to hear him speak, Jesus said to his disciples, "I have compassion for these people; they have already been with me three days and have nothing to eat. I do not want to send them away hungry, or they may collapse on the way."[134]

When contrasting the difference between the righteous and the unrighteous Jesus commended the righteous for feeding the hungry, stating: "For I was hungry and you gave me something to eat, I was thirsty and you gave me something to drink, I was a stranger and you invited me in."[135]

Feeding the hungry and giving water to the thirsty are part of our Kingdom roles and responsibilities. Johnny would probably be dead now if followers of Jesus had not heeded the call of Jesus to feed the hungry.

The Hungry of the World

Around 925 million people across the world are malnourished and go to bed desperately hungry every evening. Approximately 28,000 people per day die of hunger or hunger related causes, and at least half of these are children.[136]

Perhaps as a child you refused to eat a meal—or part of a meal—and your mother said to you, "Don't waste your food! There are millions of starving people in the world today who would love to have your meal." Often my response to this sort of statement was a trite comment such as, "Well, send it to them then!"

Of course, in this conversation my mother was using hyperbole (obvious and intentional exaggeration not to be taken literally) to teach me not to be wasteful and to appreciate the abundance of food that we enjoyed living in a wealthy nation. However, my mother's hyperbole identified one of the major challenges in feeding the hungry around the world—distribution and access.

There is more than enough food in the world to feed everyone. World agriculture produces enough calories per person per day to provide everyone in the world with the nourishment they need to be well-fed and healthy.[137] The problem in dealing with hunger is access to food for the people who most need it. The issues surrounding hunger are complex and incredibly difficult to overcome. Poverty plays a major role in hunger, as well as climate, wars, political corruption and natural disasters. But even though the issues are challenging and there are no easy, short-term solutions, this doesn't exempt us from the responsibility of doing something about world hunger.

Anyone who has the resources to feed and clothe their family and live a reasonably comfortable life, without having to worry where the next meal is coming from, has the capacity to do something for someone who is genuinely hungry. It doesn't take a lot of money to help the hungry, and there are many ways to get food to the hungry through ministries and organizations that specialize in providing food for the poor and needy in the world. We may not be able to do much, but if everyone does a "little," collectively a lot can be done.

An Overabundance of Food

Obviously, if there is enough food in the world to feed everyone, the fact that there are hungry people means that there is an unequal distribution of the food. It is a tragic injustice that in wealthy nations people have so much food that they are eating themselves to death, while in poor nations people starve to death.

The writer of the Proverbs doesn't mince words when he addresses excessive eating and drinking, stating, "Put a knife to your throat if you are given to gluttony."[138] Paul condemned the practice of the rich overindulging themselves during fellowship meals at the church while the poor went hungry.[139] Gluttony is a form of greed and self-indulgence, two things that Jesus condemned in the Pharisees: "Woe to you, teachers of the law and Pharisees, you hypocrites! You clean the outside of the cup and dish, but inside they are full of greed and self-indulgence."[140]

Very few people in developed nations really know what it is to be hungry. I have only sampled hunger when I have voluntarily chosen to fast for a limited time. In the times I have fasted I have benefited from the experience, not only because I have experienced hunger, but also because I have voluntarily gone without something that is both a pleasure and a need, for the sake of the Kingdom.

For a number of years when I was living in Australia, I participated in World Vision's 40 Hour Famine (30 Hour Famine in the United States). The idea is to go without food for 40 hours and have people sponsor you for each hour you fast. The money is then given to World Vision to provide food for the hungry. Participating in this program was a very meaningful experience. Not only was I going without food for my own spiritual edification, but also for the benefit of others. Giving up something so that others can be blessed is a basic biblical principle. Giving up food so that others who are hungry can be fed is a worthy Kingdom practice.

If we who live in wealthy nations gave up eating the additional food that we do not need—food that is making us excessively overweight and putting our health at risk—and redirected the money we spent on unhealthy overindulgence to those in the world who most need food, both those who are hungry and those of us who are overfed would benefit. This might seem like a somewhat banal comment, but consider this, the money that the average person spends each week on "junk food," which causes many of the obesity problems in developed nations, would fully sponsor Johnny in the Youth for Christ orphanage in Burundi.

Water—The World's Most Precious Resource

A couple of years ago, whilst I was visiting our ministry in Bangladesh, I travelled with some of our staff to a small village in the south. I watched as two young staff members spoke at a gathering of all the women in the village, demonstrating how they could use sugar and some other basic ingredients to treat dysentery and chronic diarrhea in children. Although a lot of water was available to these villagers, none of it was free of contamination. Our national director in Bangladesh told me that in this particular village only one in five children survived to age five, and most died from water-borne diseases. For the young mothers living in this village, their encounter with the Kingdom of God had in many cases saved the lives of their children.

At any given time, half of the world's hospital beds are occupied by patients suffering from diseases associated with lack of access to safe drinking water, inadequate sanitation and poor hygiene.[141] Around 88 percent of cases of diarrhea worldwide are attributable to unsafe water, inadequate sanitation or insufficient hygiene, and diarrhea is the second leading cause of death among children under five globally. Nearly one in five child deaths—about 1.5 million each year—is due to diarrhea. Diarrhea kills more young children than AIDS, malaria and measles combined.[142]

Over the past few years great advances in water purification technology have expanded the options and reduced the costs of providing water sanitation systems and devices for those who do not have access to clean water. It has been a great encouragement to me to meet a number of followers of Jesus who are highly qualified engineers and have given up promising careers—or given generously of their spare time—to work on solutions for providing clean water to millions of people globally.

In Matthew 10:42 we are told, "If anyone gives even a cup of cold water to one of these little ones because he is my disciple, I tell you the truth, he will certainly not lose his reward." Ensuring that people have access to clean water is something that Kingdom people should care about. And as is the case with providing food for the hungry, it is easy for those who follow Jesus to get involved. There are many organizations—both Christian and secular—that are dedicated to providing safe, clean water for those who most need it; and there are many ways that we can partner with these organizations. By simply giving a cup of cold, clean water in Jesus' name we can touch people with the Kingdom of God.

CHAPTER 8

When the Kingdom Comes . . .

MARRIAGE AND FAMILY WILL THRIVE

"Haven't you read," he replied, "that at the beginning the Creator 'made them male and female,' and said, 'For this reason a man will leave his father and mother and be united to his wife, and the two will become one flesh'? So they are no longer two, but one. Therefore what God has joined together, let man not separate." (Matthew 19:4–6)

My mobile phone was ringing again. I was in a meeting and couldn't take the call, but this was the third time it had rung. By the time I got to the end of my meeting I had six missed calls. I smiled when I saw that one of those calls was from Ben, a young leader who serves in Youth for Christ in the Midwest of the United States. I always enjoy my chats with Ben. I had met Ben at a Youth for Christ conference in South Africa. He was one of the three hundred exceptional young leaders we had selected from across the world to train, equip and empower into strategic leadership roles in the movement.

Ben was the leader of the small group that Jenny and I were a part of at the conference. It wasn't long after the conference that Ben called me and asked whether it would be okay for us to keep in touch regularly and for me to mentor him in his leadership role in Youth for Christ. I was both humbled and encouraged by his request. We place a high value on mentoring relationships in Youth for Christ and I was thrilled that I was being offered an opportunity to mentor a young leader who had so much potential.

Since the conference Ben and I had developed a close relationship through regular phone conversations and the occasional meeting. Looking at Ben's missed call on my phone I realized that I hadn't spoken to him for some time. I was eager to catch up, so I selected his name and punched the call button.

As soon as Ben answered the phone I knew that something was wrong; I could hear the distress in his voice. When I asked what was going on he shared with me some devastating news. Ben had just found out the youth pastor of his church had been having an affair with the mother of one of the young people in his youth group. He was distraught about the news.

Ben and his wife were close friends of the youth pastor and his wife. They were also very engaged in the church and had a mentoring relationship with a number of the young people and several of the church leadership. As Ben told me the impact this affair was having on the church, and in particular the young people in the youth group, I identified with his pain and disillusionment. I had seen this happen all too often.

Over the years I have served in ministry and church leadership roles there have been a number of occasions when I have had to navigate through the mess associated with extramarital affairs and/or marriage failure of leadership staff. As Ben told what he and the church were dealing with I was reminded once more of the destructive power of marital unfaithfulness. We are told in 1 Peter 5:8 that our "enemy the devil prowls around like a roaring lion looking for someone to devour." One of the most effective strategies that the devil employs to destroy the work, credibility and Kingdom-building potential of followers of Jesus is to undermine their marriage relationships.

By luring this youth pastor into an extramarital affair, the enemy had completely shut down his ministry, devastated his wife, jeopardized the well-being and future emotional and relational development of his one-year-old daughter, discredited and alienated the woman with whom he had the affair, caused untold damage to her children, generated disillusionment and distrust to varying degrees for all the young people in the church, created enormous and distracting leadership challenges for the church pastoral staff, and discredited the Kingdom of God and Jesus' reputation in the broader community.

God Hates Divorce

In Malachi 2:16 God declares that he "hates divorce." God's plan for humankind is that they marry for life. When the religious leaders pointed out to Jesus that there were provisions in the law for divorce Jesus responded:

> "It was because your hearts were hard that
> Moses wrote you this law," Jesus replied. "But at
> the beginning of creation God 'made them male
> and female.' For this reason a man will leave
> his father and mother and be united to his wife,
> and the two will become one flesh.' So they are

no longer two, but one. Therefore what God has joined together, let man not separate."[143]

When you consider the suffering and long-term and far-reaching destructive consequences of marriage breakdown, is it any wonder that God says he hates divorce and that Jesus advocates for lifelong marriage?

Long-term statistical analysis shows a direct correlation between the increase in divorce and an increase in major societal problems such as depression, substance abuse, alcoholism, violence, domestic abuse, economic stress, eating disorders and poor educational performance.[144]

According to the Bible, marriage and family are the foundational building blocks of a healthy society. In the creation story in Genesis we are told that as God surveyed what he had created each day he "saw that it was good." There is only one thing that God stated was "not good" and that was that man was alone.[145] So he created woman and then declared when he brought the woman to the man that together they truly portrayed the image of God.[146] Man and woman were made to be lifelong companions, and when they "become one" in a committed loving marriage relationship the attributes of God are portrayed and he is glorified.[147] When marriage fails the image of God is marred and the most fundamental relational foundations of society and human community are undermined.

Has the Church Capitulated?

It would be logical to assume that people of the Kingdom, who claim to follow the teachings of the Bible and practice the unconditional love of Jesus, should be far better at marriage than those who don't follow Jesus. But this does not seem to be what we see in the Church today.

The devaluing of the marriage relationship—most evident in developed and wealthy nations—seems to have infiltrated the Church to such a degree that the Kingdom of God is having little impact on the way that people conduct their marriages. According to some researchers, in Western nations, particularly in the United States, marriages are failing within the church at the same rate as outside the church.[148] In some denominations the divorce rate is higher in the church community than it is in the unchurched community.[149] Other research suggests that in churches where people are more aligned with biblical values the divorce rate is lower than that of the broader society, however it is still unacceptably high.[150]

Maintaining a marriage relationship is very difficult in an environment with many forces trying to pull marriage and family apart. It appears, from the divorce statistics for those in the Church in the United States, that the issues associated with the breakdown of marriage and family are so complex and hard to address that churches and Christian leaders have generally given up trying to prevent marriages from failing, focusing more upon dealing with the fallout of marital breakdown.

In the church's collective response to marital breakdown, the "Humpty Dumpty" principle seems to reign supreme. The age-old nursery rhyme—"Humpty Dumpty sat on the wall, Humpty Dumpty had a great fall. All the King's horses and all the King's men couldn't put Humpty together again."— describes well the approach of many local church communities to the widespread disintegration of marriages in the society in which they live and serve. As members of King Jesus' army it seems we are so preoccupied trying to piece together the shards and splinters of broken marriages that we are oblivious to the value of stopping married couples from "getting on the wall" in the first place. Surely the old adage "prevention is better than cure" applies in this case.

I have noticed that many churches in the United States have divorce recovery groups for those who have suffered marriage breakdown, but very few marriage building programs. I am not saying that divorce support groups and ministries are not needed. Much support is needed when someone is suffering the consequences of divorce and family breakdown, and people should never feel rejected by the church because of their marital status. As I have already observed, marital breakdown can cause intense emotional pain and the church needs to respond with love, acceptance and care. However, I am advocating for a far greater emphasis to be placed on keeping marriages together. Marriage and family have such high value in God's Kingdom that no effort should be spared in guarding, promoting, maintaining, nurturing and sustaining marriage.

It is not good enough to simply capitulate and say, "Oh well, that's the way things are in society, so we will just have to adapt and provide for those whose marriages have failed." As the Kingdom comes in any society it should transform the things that are contrary to Kingdom values. The love, joy, hope, grace and forgiveness of the Kingdom should infiltrate the lives of those touched by the Kingdom and transform their relationships, bringing stability and new life. In local church communities, marriage should not only have a better-than-average "survival rate," it should thrive.

Perseverance in Marriage

Many marriages fail today because the marriage relationship has been devalued to such a degree that people are no longer prepared to persevere when things get tough. The fact that more and more people are willing to give up rather than fight for their marriage indicates the diminishing value of marriage in society. And if marital breakdown in the church is as prevalent as it is in society, it indicates a diminishing value of marriage in the church.

Recent research provides conclusive evidence that people experiencing severe unhappiness and turmoil in their marriage can achieve stability, longevity and happiness by simply persevering. Amy Desai, reporting on this research in an article in Focus on the Family's online magazine, states:

> Often we think an unhappy couple has only two options:
>
> 1. Stay together and be miserable.
>
> 2. Get a divorce.
>
> But there is a third option, and many couples successfully take this other road. In an exciting new study, couples participating in a national survey were asked to rate their marriage on a scale of one to seven, with one being very unhappy and seven being very happy. Those

who rated their marriages a "one" had incredible turnarounds just five years later—if they stayed together. In fact, 77 percent of those giving their marriage a very unhappy "one" rated their marriage as a "seven" after five years. Was there some breakthrough therapy involved? No. In fact, many did relatively little—they just "stuck it out" and things got better. . . .

Another study found that about 60 percent of marriages that ended in divorce were not bad marriages, but average. They had average levels of positive interactions and average levels of conflict. Basically, these marriages were "good enough" but could be improved. Most marriages go through emotional ups and downs—times of great happiness and times of boredom and fatigue.

To have good marriages, we need to ride out the "lows" and learn from those times so that the relationship can be strengthened.[151]

Many people give up on their marriage because they don't believe it is worth enough for them to put in the effort, sacrifice or personal cost to save it. The more people value marriage the more they will be prepared to invest to save it.

One of the Church's Kingdom roles in this world should be to elevate the value of marriage to such a degree that when people in church communities go through troubling times in their marriage relationship they will be convinced that their marriage is worth saving. Marriage and family should be so highly valued by people of the Kingdom that they will be prepared to ride through storms and challenges. Followers of Jesus and the local church should be so invested in marriage that the quality of their relationships will attract the attention of all in their circles of influence. Others will be drawn to the Kingdom because they see the positive influence that Kingdom values have on marriage and family.

Unconditional Commitment to Marriage and Family

A significant component of the value drift in society that is infiltrating the Church and negatively impacting marriage relationships is the unrelenting pursuit of personal need gratification. In most marriages today, underlying the marriage commitment is an unspoken set of expectations that often include great sex, financial stability, material prosperity, romance, security, affirmation and unquestioning support of individual goals and aspirations. In the context of such expectations, marriage is in essence a formalized agreement of mutual need gratification.

When people enter into marriage expecting all their needs to be met by their spouse, they are setting themselves up for major disappointment and relational strife. Apart from the many life circumstances that work against individuals providing for all the needs of their marriage partner—children, economic stress, illness, employment demands, extended family issues, hormonal cycles, personality differences—the view that each individual's needs are paramount means that neither partner will ever be prepared or able to make the necessary sacrifices to meet the spouse's need.

I have counseled many couples whose marriages have

been in serious trouble. Whatever the presenting problems, without exception, the underlying issue identified by each marriage partner is that their needs are not being met. I have lost count of the number of times I have heard the statement, "This is not what I signed up for!" And this is a very valid statement if you entered marriage with high expectations of needs gratification.

The Bible presents unconditional selfless love as the key to meaningful relationship and fulfillment in life. But when this love is absent, fear dominates interpersonal relationships. First John 4:18 states: "There is no fear in love. But perfect love drives out fear."

When married couples base their marriage on a self-focused need-driven value system, it engenders fear rather than love. Nobody can meet all the physical, emotional, social and spiritual needs of another person. If the expectation in marriage is that every need will be met, then as each partner fails to meet the needs of his or her spouse, so each will become more disappointed and disillusioned. Eventually, one or both of the marriage partners will begin to withdraw or hold back the things that their partner is expecting or demanding, usually in retaliation for not having their own needs met. A power play ensues, with each partner either giving only so they can get something in return, or withholding something so that they can punish their partner for not giving them what they desire. The end result is a "need-bartering" relationship of fear, where the husband or wife only responds to their partner's need demands because they fear not having their own needs met. Bartering for need gratification is not a good way to conduct a marriage.

In recent times, prenuptial agreements[152] have become more common, particularly in second and third marriages. Prenuptial agreements are predicated on fear—fear of losing rather than gaining, of not having needs met and of potential pain and betrayal. Entering into a legal agreement that defines who will get what if the marriage breaks down is a recipe for failure—it is akin to signing a "death warrant" for a marriage. Prenuptial agreements are in essence declaring, "I am willing to enter the marriage as long as it doesn't cost too much; and I will remain in the marriage as long as all my needs are met. Actually, I have no real expectation that this marriage will last." It is the ultimate expression of "conditional love" and the antithesis of the selfless love of the Kingdom of God.

The antidote for fear-driven marriage relationships is the self-sacrificing love of the Kingdom of God. It is a love that only makes sense when it is freely given with no conditions attached. As the Song of Solomon declares, it is a love that cannot be bought or sold: "If a man tried to buy love with all his wealth, his offer would be utterly scorned."[153]

In a marriage relationship based upon Kingdom love, each partner is committed to giving unconditionally. Such a relationship is characterized by patience, kindness, forgiveness, selflessness and wanting the best for each other.[154] Marriage partners are not focused on having their own needs met, but rather on meeting the needs of their spouse. They give to each other not expecting anything in return—each partner constantly trying to out-give the other.

Kingdom marriage is characterized by mutual giving. It is a lifelong commitment with the expectation that there are going to be great times of fulfillment, joy and satisfaction, but also tough times—times of unhappiness and unfulfilled needs, of sacrifice and service, of disappointment and the need for grace and forgiveness. Such a marriage is untenable outside of a relationship with Jesus. For us to forego our needs for the sake of another is almost impossible from a purely human perspective. God designed us with deep longings and needs, but these needs can only ultimately be met in a relationship with Jesus.

When Jesus was conversing with the Samaritan woman at the well about her many need-driven failed relationships, he said, "Whoever drinks the water I give him will never thirst."[155] The implication was that Jesus could satisfy all her needs. In Isaiah 58:11 we are told, "The Lord will guide you always; he will satisfy your needs."

Seventeenth century French mathematician, philosopher and physicist Blaise Pascal, commenting on people's deep need for God, stated, "There is a God shaped vacuum in the heart of every man which cannot be filled by any created thing, but only by God, the Creator, made known through Jesus." In Psalm 42:1–2 David describes this God-shaped vacuum in the oft-quoted lines, "As the deer pants for streams of water, so my soul pants for you, O God. My soul thirsts for God, for the living God."

When we don't have God in our lives, instead of having our needs met by the Holy Spirit and the unwavering love of Jesus, we are constantly looking to others to meet our needs; and because nobody but God has the capacity to satisfy the deep longings of our hearts, our constant demands on others to fill the God-shaped hole in our life causes relationships to falter and fail.

Without Jesus in our life the Biblical imperative to love unconditionally is an unachievable ideal. How can we love others unconditionally when our own needs keep getting in the way? It is only when we have Jesus at the center of our life, meeting our deepest needs, that we will be completely free to give unconditionally to others without expecting or demanding anything in return.

Selfless, unconditionally loving marriage grounded in a need-satisfying relationship with Jesus is a wonderful gift that followers of Jesus are able to model to those outside his Kingdom. However, the capacity of believers to help others to experience this gift is very closely tied to the Church's ability to successfully foster and promote God-honoring marriage.

Proactive Marriage Support

Nurturing and supporting marriage and family, and fighting against the forces in the world that are designed by the devil to tear marriages apart, should be high on the list of priorities for any church. Kingdom-oriented churches should deliberately, strategically and publicly commit to marriage and family, communicating to all in the church that they are going to do everything they can to ensure that marriages prosper and grow; and that this commitment to marriage is going to be reflected in all program and budget decisions.

There are many ways that Kingdom communities can invest in marriage and family: marriage enrichment programs, marriage retreats, counseling services, teaching on marriage and family and premarital preparation courses and counseling. An abundance of biblically-based, effective Kingdom-honoring marriage building programs and materials are available to churches to help strengthen marriages and support families. Much can be done, but it will take a deliberate and concerted effort by church leaders and church communities to redress the trends of marital failure and family stress in the Church.

Prayer for marriages

The destabilization and dismantling of marriage and family is one of the most effective strategies that Satan uses to destroy the testimony and service potential of believers and frustrate the work of the Church. In fighting for the sanctity and health of marriages we need to consider the spiritual dimensions of this battle and employ the spiritual weapons at our disposal. In passages of the Bible that address the subject of spiritual warfare, prayer is identified as the most powerful weapon available to us. In Ephesians 6:18, after listing the armor of God, Paul sums up his directives on spiritual warfare by stating: "And pray in the Spirit on all occasions with all kinds of prayers and requests. With this in mind, be alert and always keep on praying for all the saints."

Concerted and dedicated prayer should be an essential element of the Church's marriage and family ministry.

Preparation: premarital counseling

I am greatly encouraged by the number of churches that provide premarital counseling for couples who are seeking to marry. Formal biblically-based marriage preparation goes a long way toward ensuring that marriages begin well. Many effective tools to help prepare people for marriage focus on realistic expectations, unconditional love, communication, mutual respect, honesty and transparency and other vital foundational aspects of a Kingdom-based marriage.

Prevention: fitness plans for marriage

Investing in marriage enrichment courses, married couple retreats, marriage growth programs and social events for couples validates marriage, promotes health and helps identify potential problems so they can be addressed before they become major destructive issues.

I recently visited a church that encouraged married couples in their congregation to go through a twenty-four-month marriage building course. More than half the married couples in the church participated and the impact on families and marriages was significant. Many reported that the program had radically improved their marriage, brought them much closer together as a couple and helped them identify and deal with potentially destructive flaws in their relationship.

Respite for parents

One of the things a local church community is well equipped to provide is respite for parents, particularly those with young children. Caring for a couple's children so that they can have a "date night"—some time on their own for communication, romance, relaxation and restoration—is a gift that is easily given and one that has significant potential to strengthen a marriage relationship.

Greater respite support may be needed for those couples who are struggling in their marriage and need to participate in extended counseling or a marriage restoration retreat. But most churches are more than able to respond to longer-term respite needs of married couples, particularly if the whole church community is dedicated to marriage and family.

Mentoring

Encouraging older married couples who have healthy, godly marriages to mentor younger couples is another way to support and nurture marriage and family in the church. This can be informal, with a general challenge given by church leadership to older couples to offer to mentor and support younger couples; or it can be an organized program, allocating a number of younger couples to each older couple.

Jenny and I have been involved in various churches and Christian communities where we have had opportunity to invest in the lives of other married couples, mostly younger than us and newer in their faith. We have been greatly encouraged as we have seen couples strengthened and nurtured in their marriages. The surprising byproduct of investing in other couples' marriages was that our own marriage was strengthened. As we ministered to others it enabled us to review and celebrate our relationship and revisit important lessons that shaped our marriage.

Married couples who have successfully navigated the marriage journey over many years are able to offer two valuable treasures to younger couples: hope and wisdom. Hope that it is possible to not only "survive" the tough times, but to grow through them; and wisdom that comes from both positive and negative experiences, and that allows an older couple to share what worked for them, identify and empathize with what younger couples are experiencing and provide solidarity and counsel.

Restoration: marriage counseling

Developing supportive networks and counseling resources

at a local level is essential if a church is serious about stemming the tide of marital failure. When a marriage gets into trouble the church needs to be able to respond with competent support and dedicated resources, providing counseling services either internally or through an arrangement with a marriage counseling ministry.

Dedicating staff and resources

Something as important and strategic as the nurture of marriage and family and combating marital breakdown warrants the prioritized allocation of staff and resources. Whether a church is large with multiple staff, or small with one full-time pastor and volunteer leaders, all churches have the capacity to identify leaders and allocate time and finances to provide marriage and family initiatives.

It really is an issue of priorities and values. Allocation of resources reflects the values of a church. With marriage and family being such a high priority in God's Kingdom, every church should have someone in its senior leadership dedicated to the development, nurture and pastoral support of marriage and family.

A Haven for Marriage and Family

I used to own a small sailing boat. Because of the limited time I had available I would take the boat out as often as I could. One day, when the forecast was not good, I ventured out regardless.

When I arrived at the beach the weather was perfect for sailing—sunny, steady off-shore breeze, low swell and little chop. I wasn't too concerned about the forecast—the forecasters often got it wrong anyway—but I decided I wouldn't venture too far off shore, just in case the weather turned. I was about a mile out when the sun was suddenly blocked by heavy clouds. The wind started to pick up and white caps formed on top of the waves. I tacked and started heading for shore, but before I got very far a massive squall hit me. My fifteen-foot sailing dingy was a "trapeze" boat with a huge sail area. The wind was so strong that my friend who was crewing for me that day and I both had to be fully extended on our trapeze harnesses just to keep the boat from capsizing. Eight-foot waves were pounding over the boat and we couldn't see more than a few feet in front of us. However, when the storm hit us I had been heading toward shore, so I just tried to keep the boat pointed in that general direction.

All of a sudden there was a brief lull in the storm, just enough for me to see a little bay off the port bow with a small opening. The weather quickly closed over again, but I had a good bearing on where that bay entrance was and I sailed for it with all the skill and ability I had at my disposal.

Saturated, shivering cold, eyes stinging, every muscle screaming for relief, we finally made it to the bay entrance and sailed through. The change in conditions was amazing. One minute we were battling with everything we had to keep the boat upright and on course, and the next we were in calm, almost flat waters. The bay was so well protected from the elements by the surrounding cliffs that it shut off the intensity of the storm. We had inadvertently found a "haven," and it had saved us from potential disaster.

The word *haven* means "a place of shelter and safety; refuge; sanctuary, security." When I was caught in that storm, battered by the destructive forces around me, I desperately needed a haven, and as soon as I saw that little bay, I sailed for it, longing for the security and calm it offered. The Church should be a haven for marriage and family; a prominent shelter from the destructive forces trying to capsize marriages and drown them in despair; a place of security and protection. And when families navigate into that haven, they should be overwhelmed with the peace, love, care and nurture that can only be found in the Kingdom of God.

CHAPTER 9

THE PREREQUISITES FOR KINGDOM GROWTH

But you will receive power when the Holy Spirit comes on you; and you will be my witnesses in Jerusalem, and in all Judea and Samaria, and to the ends of the earth. (Acts 1:8)

In India more than 4,000 new churches were established in Madhya Pradesh State in a seven year period, with around 50,000 new believers. In Orissa during the 1990's a new church was planted every 24 hours. After 50 years of practically no mission success amongst Bhojpuri-speaking people, in a five year period 4,000 new churches were established with 300,000 new believers.

In China more than 30,000 believers are baptized every day. In the Qing'an County 236 churches were planted in a single month and in 2001 a provincial church planting movement produced 48,000 new believers and 1,700 new churches in one year.

161

In Africa over the past century the number
of professing Christians has grown from nine
million to 360 million. Each month 1,200 new
churches are started.

And after years of rejection of the Gospel
90,000 of Kenya's 600,000 Maasai have recently
become followers of Jesus.

In the Muslim world more Muslims have come
to Christ in the past two decades than at any
other time in history. In North Africa, over
16,000 Berbers have come to Christ, and in
an Asian Muslim nation more than 150,000
Muslims have become Christians and now meet
in more than 3,000 locally led Isa Jamaats (Jesus
Groups).

In Europe a significant movement amongst
the Gypsy people in France and Spain saw the
Gypsy church grow from 10,000 to 150,000 in a
15 year period.

In Colombia every Saturday night 18,000 youth
gather in Bogotá and at least 500 youth at each
gathering commit their lives to Christ and
the core values of prayer, fasting and holiness.
During the week they meet in 8,000 youth cell
groups.

These accounts of exceptional advances of the Kingdom of God are recorded in a groundbreaking book by David Garrison titled *Church Planting Movements: How God is Redeeming a Lost World*.[156] Garrison cites many examples of phenomenal church growth, and then through careful analysis of each example, identifies the fundamental characteristics and values that are common to all: extraordinary prayer, abundant evangelism, intentional planting of reproducing churches, the authority of God's Word, local leadership, lay leadership, house churches, churches planting churches, rapid reproduction and healthy churches.[157]

In his book *Movements that Changed the World*, Steve Addison examines the nature and uniqueness of movements of God that have significantly impacted the world and identifies five key characteristics that are endemic to all of these movements: white-hot faith, commitment to a cause, contagious relationships, rapid mobilization and adaptive methods.[158]

In the year 2000 Youth for Christ was in a difficult place. We came to the realization that we had largely lost our way. We had lost sight of the fact that Youth for Christ was a movement of God and over several years had tried to fix serious leadership and spiritual problems with organizational theory and practice. With nowhere else to go, we were brought to our knees before God and through a three-year period of deep soul searching, godly leadership, concerted and dedicated prayer, brokenness, honesty before God and dependency on the Holy Spirit's guidance, our movement was renewed. God gave us a new set of "marching orders"—foundational values and characteristics that defined who God wanted us to be, essentials necessary for growing his Kingdom and following his call and vision for the movement. We were directed to be: prayer dependent, evangelistically focused, discipleship oriented (making reproducing disciples), biblically based, pioneering spirited, servant led and interdependent. We were also given a very clear mandate from God to empower young people and allow them to lead the movement. Wherever we have comprehensively applied these values and directives we have seen unprecedented growth in the movement and great advances of the Kingdom, particularly in regions of the world that are considered hostile to Christians and resistant to the gospel.

The above examples, along with many other studies of Christian revivals and movements of God over the past two centuries, identify a number of characteristics foundational to all significant advances of God's Kingdom:

- Extraordinary prayer
- Brokenness, repentance and dependency upon God
- Commitment to evangelism
- Submission to the authority of God's Word
- Godly servant-hearted leadership
- Sacrificial service to others
- The centrality and preeminence of Jesus

Extraordinary Prayer

Listening to God

Prayer is communication and communion with God. It is the means by which we share our life with Jesus and provide him with the opportunity to speak to us and direct our ways.

If we want to be involved in the work of the Kingdom and serve Jesus effectively, then it is essential that we communicate with him regularly and consistently. The less people pray, the less they are dependent upon God and the more they are dependent upon their own wisdom and expertise. By constantly and deliberately taking all our decisions and plans before God and seeking his input, we are acknowledging his sovereignty and our subservience to his will and instruction.

If we do not have prayer as a foundational value and practice of our life and service we are declaring to God—and the world around us—that we do not need him. A capable, gifted leader can do a whole lot without God, but such a leader will achieve little for the Kingdom and is incredibly vulnerable to catastrophic failure. As Christian communities become more sophisticated and institutionalized there is a corresponding inherent danger of becoming reliant upon the skills, ability and knowledge of leaders and the capacity of systems to deliver what is necessary to serve God and his Kingdom. Self-reliant leaders—people who lean more on their gifts, skills, influence and personal resources than they do on God—think they do not need to consult with God and prayer is generally not a big part of their ministry; they are literally saying to God, "I've got this covered, Lord; I'll call on you when I need you."

A significant distinctive of exceptional world-changing movements is their absolute dependency upon God expressed in dedicated, daily and consistent prayer accompanied by humble leadership with strong accountability structures and a high sensitivity to the Holy Spirit's leading.

Prayer is as much about listening as it is about telling, and it involves far more than presenting God with a shopping list of requests or telling God of our plans and aspirations and asking for his blessing upon what we have decided to do. Our prayer life should be epitomized by the words of Psalm 139:23: "Search me, O God, and know my heart; test me and know my anxious thoughts. See if there is any offensive way in me, and lead me in the way everlasting."

In Proverbs 3:5–6 we are told, "Trust in the Lord with all your heart and lean not on your own understanding; in all your ways acknowledge him, and he will make your paths straight." If we are not constantly consulting with God in prayer and seeking his guidance, then by necessity we will have to plan and live by our own wisdom, and on the occasions that we do pray, we will find ourselves presenting God with our plans and seeking his endorsement. By "leaning on our own understanding" we may end up with amazing physical structures and well-resourced organizations with highly capable leaders, but in most likelihood what we have built will only be a testimony or monument to our own abilities; one that has little to do with the Kingdom of God.

An act of obedience

Jesus says in John 14:15, "If you love me, you will obey what I command." In 1 Samuel 15:22 we read, "To obey is better than sacrifice." Being obedient to God is essential if we wish to serve in his Kingdom. Prayer is an act of obedience.

Throughout God's Word we are commanded to pray. It is not an optional exercise. It is an expression of our faithfulness and obedience to Jesus. If we choose not to pray, then we are disobeying a direct instruction from our Lord. For example, in

1 Thessalonians 5:17 we are commanded to "pray continually." And in Ephesians 6:18 we are instructed to "pray in the Spirit on all occasions with all kinds of prayers and requests. With this in mind, be alert and always keep on praying for all the saints."

When Jesus gave us the Lord's Prayer he didn't say "if" you pray, he said "when" you pray (Matthew 6:5–15). The expectation of Jesus is that prayer will be an integral part of the life of his followers. We cannot serve effectively in God's Kingdom and downgrade prayer to an optional extra that we engage in only when we have time or have nowhere else to turn.

Powerful and effective

Does prayer make a difference? When we pray, do things happen? Can prayer influence the course of history and impact the course of our lives and the lives of others? According to God's Word prayer can and does influence the circumstances and outcomes of human life and world affairs. In James 5:16 we read that "the prayer of a righteous man is powerful and effective."

There are endless examples in biblical and Church history of the intervention of God in the affairs of humankind in response to the prayers of his followers. James uses the example of Elijah in establishing that prayer is a powerful tool that is available to any believer: "Elijah was a man just like us. He prayed earnestly that it would not rain, and it did not rain on the land for three and a half years. Again he prayed, and the heavens gave rain, and the earth produced its crops."[159]

I think one of the reasons we don't pray is that we doubt

our prayers make any difference. Do we really believe that God can miraculously intervene in the affairs of humankind because of our prayers? Unfortunately, if we never really venture out in prayer—not only the casual "emergency" prayer, but deeply involving prayer that is grounded in faith and seeks God's will—then we are never going to be convinced that God can answer prayer because we will never have firsthand evidence that he does.

The story I shared in Chapter 4 about purchasing the house next door to the church was a story of answered prayer. When the hostile owner offered to sell us his property on the very day and at the very moment I had decided to approach him to ask him if he would be willing to sell his house, it was clearly an act of God in response to our prayer. We were convinced through much prayer and consultation with God that he wanted us to have that house, and so we were able to step out in faith, acting on our prayer, and in doing so saw God's miraculous answer to what we asked of him. I think God answered our prayers in such a way that there would be no doubt that it was only because of him that we were able to acquire the house, so that when he later directed us to use the house to accommodate homeless young people, there was no resistance to his direction.

As we pray, seek God's will, take steps of faith and see the Lord answer prayer, it opens the door for God "to do immeasurably more than all we ask or imagine."[160]

Alignment with God's will

Prayer can have a huge impact in the lives of believers and those they pray for, but there are conditions to our prayers being effective. One of the most common misunderstandings about prayer is the view that prayer is a means to get God to do something for us. We see things in our life that we don't like, issues that are adversely affecting us, things that we think God should be doing, options that would make life easier for us and others; and we ask God to intervene on our behalf, often projecting on him the outcome we expect.

However, prayer is not about us and our agenda. Prayer is first and foremost an alignment of our will with the will of God, as opposed to aligning God's will with ours. Seeking God's will is a prerequisite to effective prayer. First John 5:14 states, "This is the confidence we have in approaching God: that if we ask anything according to his will, he hears us."

God's will is primarily revealed in the Bible. For any prayer to be effective it must first align with the truths and values of the Bible. When we pray, it should be in the context of the establishment of God's Kingdom values in our life and in the world around us—that God's "will be done on earth as it is in heaven." Beyond this, we can also seek God's "specific" will through prayer, and as God reveals his will for us we can continue to pray according to what he reveals, aligning our decisions and life direction with his specific purpose and plan for us. An important thing to remember, though, is that God's specific will for us will never contradict his universal values, character and will as expressed in his Word.

The prayer life of Jesus

Jesus modeled a life of prayer. In the Gospel accounts Jesus' life and ministry is infused with prayer. When Jesus walked this earth he spent much time in solitude with his

Father—often all night—particularly in moments of major decisions and ministry challenge. Jesus' prayer life was focused on seeking his Father's direction and will, rather than asking his Father to do things for him:

> I tell you the truth, the Son can do nothing by himself; he can do only what he sees his Father doing, because whatever the Father does the Son also does. For the Father loves the Son and shows him all he does. (John 5:19–20)

> For I did not speak of my own accord, but the Father who sent me commanded me what to say and how to say it. I know that his command leads to eternal life. So whatever I say is just what the Father has told me to say. (John 12:49–50)

> Father, if you are willing, take this cup from me; yet not my will, but yours be done. (Luke 22:42)

Jesus calls those who would follow him to live as he lived.[161] Self-denying prayer was a pivotal and vital part of Jesus' life and ministry on this earth, and he asks nothing less of us. If we are authentically following Jesus, then our daily walk should be infused with self-denying prayer focused on seeking God's will and way in every aspect of life.

Faith is the foundation
Believing in God's capacity to answer is another key

element to effective prayer. In James 1:5–7 we are told, "If any of you lacks wisdom, he should ask God, who gives generously to all without finding fault, and it will be given to him. But when he asks, he must believe and not doubt, because he who doubts is like a wave of the sea, blown and tossed by the wind. That man should not think he will receive anything from the Lord."

This faith element of prayer is grounded in a recognition and acknowledgment of the person we are praying to. We are praying to the creator of the universe—the sovereign and all-powerful God—and for our prayers to be effective we must in faith believe that God can and will answer our prayer according to his will. Recognizing that we are praying to the God of the impossible enables us to pray for the impossible. As Jesus explained to his disciples when they were wrestling with the inclusiveness of the Kingdom, "With man this is impossible, but not with God; all things are possible with God."[162]

Spiritual warfare and prayer

One of the "mysteries" of prayer is that when we pray things happen in the spiritual realm that are largely beyond our limited worldview and human understanding. When Jesus' disciples failed to drive out a demon, Jesus explained to them that their failure was due to a lack of prayer.[163] Any advancement of the Kingdom of God is going to involve spiritual warfare, and without prayer we are going to be ineffective in battling the incredibly powerful forces aligned against us.

The concept of prayer being a vital weapon in spiritual warfare is found in Ephesians 6:12 where we are told that "our struggle is not against flesh and blood, but against the rulers, against the authorities, against the powers of this dark world and against the spiritual forces of evil in the heavenly realms." To combat these spiritual forces we are instructed to put on the full armor of God and employ this armor by praying "in the Spirit on all occasions with all kinds of prayers and requests."[164]

The value of corporate prayer

Corporate prayer is also vital as we do battle for the Kingdom. We are told by Jesus that "if two of you on earth agree about anything you ask for, it will be done for you by my Father in heaven. For where two or three come together in my name, there am I with them."[165] As we agree together in the context of Christian community, the impact of our prayers extends beyond the physical realm in which we live and allows us to engage in the affairs of heaven. In corporate prayer there is the potential for a greater sense of God's presence and a greater sensitivity to his direction and will as we interact and fellowship with each other and encounter Jesus in and through the lives of those we join with in prayer.

The Kingdom of God is about community, about discovering God in each other, serving one another and combining our gifts to portray Jesus and do God's will. It is through our love for each other that the world will see and be drawn to Jesus. Followers of Jesus have far greater strength and potential as a united force than they have on their own. There is enormous strategic value in gathering followers of Jesus together to pray. However, corporate prayer has nothing to do with using prayer as a currency to buy God's favor; that the more people we get praying the more we can convince God to respond. Rather, it is the mobilization of God's people to do battle in a spiritual dimension where prayer has significant implications for our capacity to overcome the enemy, advance God's Kingdom and protect and empower God's people.

Caring through prayer

Praying for others shows that you care for them. Occasionally when I am in a restaurant with some fellow believers I will say to the server when he or she takes the order for the meal, "We are followers of Jesus and we pray before we eat thanking God for the meal. We want to pray for you—is there anything that you would like us to pray for?" Invariably the initial answer given is that there is nothing in particular that our server would like us to pray for. But almost without exception, after a short while the server returns and shares with us some specific need or issues for us to pray about. I have sometimes had servers in tears standing by our table as we have prayed for them and their family and the issue that they are dealing with.

I will not easily forget the time I was sitting in a restaurant of a hotel in East Africa with the National Director of the Youth for Christ ministry in that nation. A woman entered the restaurant and my colleague identified her as a government minister. He immediately walked over to her and introduced himself. She acknowledged that she knew who he was and he told her that he had been praying for her. She asked what he had been specifically praying for. He replied: "I know that you have recently been through a painful divorce and I have been praying that you will find someone who will genuinely love and care for you and whom you can love." I could see that she was deeply moved and with misty eyes she asked my friend if he had been praying for anything else for her. He replied, "I have been praying that you would find a personal relationship with Jesus." To this she answered, "That prayer has already been answered. I gave my life to Jesus last week."

Do we care enough to pray for others? Prayer not only changes lives but it conveys to those we pray for that they matter to us and to God.

Prayer as a priority

Prayer should be prominent, central and highly valued in any community that desires to serve God and advance his Kingdom. If prayer is a priority, it will be reflected in the allocation of leadership and organizational resources.

When we had reached the end of ourselves in Youth for Christ and humbly sought God's direction as to what we needed to do to get back on track, he told us that we needed to make prayer the foundation of our movement and ministry. One of our first responses to this directive was to appoint an international prayer director. We then went on to encourage each of our national ministries to appoint a prayer director.

Since her appointment, our international prayer director, along with many of the national prayer leaders, has introduced many innovative prayer initiatives and we now have prayer strategies for young people, women, men, young leaders, ministry partners/donors, mothers, national and international leaders, staff and volunteers. Through the prioritizing of prayer and the subsequent allocation of leadership we have gone from having no coordinated global prayer strategy to now having more than 220,000 registered prayer intercessors who pray for our ministry and the young people of the world daily and who can be mobilized through our prayer networks to prayer for immediate and crucial prayer needs, as well as major ministry initiatives.

Dismissing prayer as something that doesn't work because people don't support or attend a midweek prayer meeting or the occasional prayer service is not valid. When prayer is treated by a church leadership as an afterthought, then it is little wonder the church community doesn't respond well to invitations to pray. Local churches serious about advancing the Kingdom of God should have someone in a senior leadership role who is a champion for prayer and who oversees a broad array of prayer strategies that engage and mobilize all segments of the church community. There is a wide range of innovative and culturally relevant initiatives, programs and processes available that can be employed to encourage and mobilize people to pray, many of which leverage the power of modern communication mediums such as the internet and electronic media.

Brokenness, Repentance and Dependency upon God

The revival that swept across America in the nineteenth century led by Charles Finney resulted in the most "conversions" of any Christian movement in the United States since the founding of the nation. Finney's preaching and advocacy for authentic and radical faith was so influential that he became known as the "Father of Modern Revivalism."[166] Whenever he preached, Finney's starting point was repentance. He believed that personal repentance always preceded an outpouring of God's Spirit and was foundational to any genuine advancement of the Kingdom of God.

Finney's perspective on repentance is founded upon and validated by the teaching of Jesus and the apostles:

> From that time on Jesus began to preach,
> "Repent, for the kingdom of heaven is near."
> (Matthew 4:17)

> "The time has come," he said. "The kingdom of God is near. Repent and believe the good news!" (Mark 1:15)

> They went out and preached that people should repent. (Mark 6:12)

> But unless you repent, you too will all perish. (Luke 13:5)

> I tell you that in the same way there will be more rejoicing in heaven over one sinner who repents than over ninety-nine righteous persons who do not need to repent. (Luke 15:7)

> Peter replied, "Repent and be baptized, every one of you, in the name of Jesus Christ for the forgiveness of your sins. And you will receive the gift of the Holy Spirit." (Acts 2:38)

> Repent, then, and turn to God, so that your sins

may be wiped out, that times of refreshing may
come from the Lord. (Acts 3:19)

Remember the height from which you have
fallen! Repent and do the things you did at
first. If you do not repent, I will come to you
and remove your lampstand from its place.
(Revelation 2:5)

Genuine repentance always results in radical life change
and is driven by an overwhelming sense of God's holiness,
but also of his love and grace. It involves an encounter with
God wherein a person is confronted through the work of
the Holy Spirit with who he is, what he believes and where
he stands with God. In the stark reality of a new awareness
of inadequacy, sin and deep need for forgiveness, the person
responds to the invitation of Jesus to follow him.

According to the NIV Bible Dictionary, "repentance
is a profound change of mind involving the changing
of the direction of life from that of self-centeredness or
sin-centeredness to God- or Christ-centeredness. God's
forgiveness is available only to those who are repentant, for
only they can receive it."[167]

Repentance occurs when someone is truly broken
before God; when a person realizes the desperate need of a
relationship with Jesus because we cannot in our own strength
"redeem" ourselves and be the people we deep down long
to be—the people God has designed us to be. Repentance
involves yielding control of your life to God; moving from self-
sufficiency to a total dependence upon God, recognizing the

sovereignty of God in your life and surrendering everything to him—gifts, talents, ambitions, career, possessions, money, relationships, values and priorities. Repentance is a necessary and foundational prerequisite for Kingdom membership and for effective Kingdom ministry.

Commitment to Evangelism

In Acts 1:8 we find a definitive evangelical prophecy and directive of Jesus for his disciples and his church: "But you will receive power when the Holy Spirit comes on you; and you will be my witnesses in Jerusalem, and in all Judea and Samaria, and to the ends of the earth."

Acting on this vision and commission to evangelize the world, eleven men along with a few hundred other followers of Jesus initiated a movement that now has around 2.1 billion adherents in the world today. And it has been simple, faithful, sold-out-to-Jesus people who have populated the various movements throughout history and generated exceptional growth that has impacted the world and resulted in billions coming to faith in Jesus. The common characteristic of all these growth-producing believers has been their unwavering commitment to evangelism—to sharing Jesus with the world.

I have already said much about evangelism and the Gospel in Chapter 2, but suffice it to say that God doesn't want "anyone to perish, but everyone to come to repentance."[168] Our alignment with the imperative of the Lord's Prayer that "God's will be done" must include a commitment to provide everyone in this world an opportunity to be a follower of Jesus, to offer the Kingdom of God to all.

A genuine encounter with Jesus should result in an

unquenchable desire to share Jesus with others. When Paul is talking about what drives him to evangelize he says, "For Christ's love compels us, because we are convinced that one died for all, and therefore all died. And he died for all, that those who live should no longer live for themselves but for him who died for them and was raised again."[169] "I am compelled to preach. Woe to me if I do not preach the gospel!"[170] I believe that what Paul is saying is "Jesus died for all but all don't yet know that; so I am not going to rest until everyone knows that Jesus died for them, rose from the dead and wants them to have the life that only he can provide."

Paul was prepared to do anything, be anything, suffer anything and give anything so that others might know Jesus. Are we prepared to do the same?

Submission to the Authority of God's Word

David Garrison identified the vital role God's Word plays in the sustainability of a world changing movement of God:

> As Church Planting Movements produce
> multiple reproducing churches, what keeps the
> movement from fragmenting into thousands
> of heresies like a crack splintering across a car
> windshield? There can only be one answer: the
> Authority of God's word. Like an invisible
> spinal cord aligning and supporting the
> movement, there runs through each Church
> Planting Movement a commitment to the
> authority of the Bible.[171]

I am sure that it is obvious by now that I view the Bible as the primary source for assessing the will of God for me and any who would follow Jesus. I have used the Bible extensively throughout this book to validate and substantiate my position on the many aspects of Kingdom living I have so far addressed.

Endemic to all great movements of the Kingdom is an unshakable commitment to the authority of the Word of God. The Bible is seen as the truth in its entirety and studying, reading, sharing, learning, applying and referencing the Bible is intrinsic to effective and God-honoring ministry and mission. Any wavering from this position generally results in one or more of the following: confusion of belief, distortion of truth, lack of integrity, secularism, division and disunity, diminishing commitment to the gospel, cultural impositions, universalism, legalism and exclusivism.

Biblical illiteracy

The pervasive decline in biblical literacy and the diminishing acknowledgment of the authority of the Bible throughout the Church globally is a huge concern, particularly when we consider how essential biblical knowledge and the respect of biblical authority is to the vibrancy and health of Kingdom-advancing movements.

Recent research in the United States has revealed some very disturbing trends in the Church. George Barna, reporting on his investigation of biblical literacy in the Church in America, says:

> The Christian body in America is immersed
> in a crisis of biblical illiteracy. How else can

you describe matters when most churchgoing
adults reject the accuracy of the Bible, reject the
existence of Satan, claim that Jesus sinned, see
no need to evangelize, believe that good works
are one of the keys to persuading God to forgive
their sins, and describe their commitment to
Christianity as moderate or even less firm?[172]

Barna further reports on some other disturbing facts:

The most widely known Bible verse among
adult and teen believers is "God helps those who
help themselves"—which is not actually in the
Bible and conflicts with the basic message of
Scripture.

Less than one out of every ten believers
possess a biblical worldview as the basis for his
or her decision-making or behavior.

When given thirteen basic teachings
from the Bible, only 1% of adult believers
firmly embraced all thirteen as being biblical
perspectives.[173]

The provision of access to the Bible for the "ordinary
believer" was the catalyst for the Protestant Reformation that
ushered in a golden era of church growth, mission, revival
and evangelical endeavor. Up until Martin Luther translated
the Bible into the language of the common people, the only
Bible available was the Latin translation, which was for the
exclusive use of the clergy of the church.

When the general population in Germany gained access to the Bible in their own language they were able to study the Scriptures for themselves, discover the truth and apply it to their lives. It had a tremendous impact on the church and on German culture. As people started to live and serve under the authority of God's Word rather than the authority of the Roman Catholic priests, it not only impacted Germany and the surrounding nations, but also led to the production of the Geneva Bible and then the King James Bible, which in turn generated a revolution in the English-speaking Church. Authentic, Bible-believing missional churches sprang up all over Europe and formed the foundation for great advancement of God's Kingdom.

Is it time for another "reformational" connection of those in the Church to the authority and truth of God's Word? It would seem so. Although we have an amazing abundance of biblical literature, translations, study guides and devotionals, it appears that fewer and fewer people are reading God's Word and applying to their lives. We seem to have slipped back into the pre-reformation practice where "professional" leaders of the church are the only ones who have an intimate knowledge of the Bible and are interpreting it for the masses.

Today's Church has many sound teachers and biblical expositors, but also many misguided, unbiblical, self-focused purveyors of so-called biblical truth who are teaching and practicing self-serving, materialistic and/or "comfortable" expressions of church that have nothing to do with the Kingdom of God or authentic, self-denying faith in Jesus. The only effective counter to this theological drift is to get people personally reconnected to the content, authority and truth of God's Word.

The truth and authority of God's Word

It is not only a problem of biblical illiteracy that we are facing today but also a lack of respect for the authority and all-encompassing truth of the Bible. Although there is still much to be done in the world to provide God's Word to all people groups in their own language and culture, a large majority of people around the world today have access to the Bible in their language. The Bible is the best-selling book in the world every year and easily the best-selling book of all time. According to author Russell Ash in his book titled *The Top 10 of Everything*, "No one really knows how many copies of the Bible have been printed, sold, or distributed. The Bible Society's attempt to calculate the number printed between 1816 and 1975 produced the figure of 2,458,000,000. A more recent survey, for the years up to 1992, put it closer to 6,000,000,000 in more than 2,000 languages and dialects. Whatever the precise figure, the Bible is by far the bestselling book of all time."[174]

In the United States more than 25 million Bibles are sold every year, however, as Barna and others have shown, fewer and fewer people are reading the Bible and applying it to their lives. I think this has a lot to do with the declining respect people have for the Bible.

Many in the Church today no longer believe that the Bible is in its entirety "the truth"—the revelation of God to humankind. The Bible is seen as a collection of writings that contains "some truth"—that has some value in helping people to know and understand God—but mainly consists of the opinions and thoughts of men, and as such, the imperatives, commands, values and principles in the Bible are subjectively questioned.

When the Bible is treated as a "reference book" rather than the truth from God that transcends all human wisdom, then there is far less reason for people to read God's Word and apply it to their lives. With the downgrading of the Bible to just another book that has some value in guiding one through life, the imperative for those in the Church to study and know the Scriptures competes on equal footing with all the other demands on people's time and attention, often getting pushed down to the bottom of the list of "things to do when we have time to get to them."

The Bible is unequivocal in its declaration that it is, in its entirety, the Word of God to humankind and the ultimate authority for all those who would follow Jesus and serve in God's Kingdom:

> All Scripture is God-breathed and is useful for teaching, rebuking, correcting and training in righteousness, so that the man of God may be thoroughly equipped for every good work.[175]

> Above all, you must understand that no prophecy of Scripture came about by the prophet's own interpretation. For prophecy never had its origin in the will of man, but men spoke from God as they were carried along by the Holy Spirit.[176]

Jesus constantly used Scripture to validate his ministry and identity and to teach people the truth of God.[177] He stated that "the Scripture can not be broken"[178] and that his ministry was a "fulfillment of Scripture."[179] In John 5:39 he said to the Jewish leaders, "You diligently study the Scriptures because you think that by them you possess eternal life. These are the Scriptures that testify about me."

The Apostles also consistently declared the Scriptures to be the authority by which they lived and the reference point for their service in the Kingdom.[180]

If Jesus and the Apostles treated Scripture as the unquestionable truth of God, then those who follow him and serve in his Kingdom should do the same.

Taking people to God's Word

As mentioned in Chapter 1, one of the best ways to help people appreciate God's Word is to take them to it rather than interpret it for them or quote it to them. Those of us who know and respect the authority of the Bible should always look for opportunities to encourage others to read, study and apply God's Word for themselves. When we are asked for advice or counsel, rather than telling people what is in the Bible or administering biblical truth to their life, let's instead take them to the Bible and read it with them and together discover God's truth and direction.

In Acts 17 the Bereans were commended for assessing the veracity of Paul's teaching by checking for themselves how it aligned with God's Word: "Now the Bereans were of more noble character than the Thessalonians, for they received the message with great eagerness and examined the Scriptures every day to see if what Paul said was true."[181] Apart from their diligence in searching God's Word to validate Paul's message, what is also implied is that the Bereans studied the Scriptures together.

Common to all vibrant Kingdom movements is not only a respect for the authority of the Bible but a commitment to collectively study and apply the truth of God's Word to the life and values of the believer. This is consistently achieved in small groups where people come together to study the Bible on a regular basis with strong values of mutual accountability and transparency.

Small groups are one of the best environments for exploring and applying God's Word. In the intimacy of a small group people have the opportunity to build trust and in the context of that trust to share honestly and candidly with each other. In a healthy small group people feel safe to share the struggles and challenges of life as well as their doubts and questions of faith and belief. As the group grapples with the "stuff of life," the Word comes alive and the relevance and truth of Scripture are affirmed as it is applied to the issues and unique life situations of each of the members of the group.

Oral learners

Many traditional cultures in the world don't communicate or learn through written words. Along with these, today's emerging globalized youth culture is exhibiting a propensity toward an "oral" rather than a literate text-based "read and study" learning style. Rather than reading books, studies, reference material, magazines and newspapers, oral learners communicate and receive and process information through stories, visual media, songs and drama.

When we are considering the challenges of sharing the Gospel globally and providing opportunity for all people to study and apply God's Word, it is very important that we recognize that more than half the world's people are illiterate oral learners. In addition to the traditional or primary oral learners, it needs to be noted that a vast majority of globalized youth are "secondary oral learners," in that they are functionally literate but acquire their information and entertainment primarily from the electronic media.

We need to be extremely creative to reach and serve the oral learners of this world. Many mission and ministry organizations are developing films, tapes, CDs, blogs, computer-based animated and interactive programs, and web-based media to effectively communicate with primary and secondary oral learners. These resources are available to the Church globally, but unfortunately, it seems that many local churches, particularly in developed nations, are locked into a print-based communication and learning style.

A leading authority on oral cultures, Rick Brown, explains how important it is for print-based learners to understand and adapt their communication style to effectively share the gospel with oral learners:

> Since people learn best when information
> is presented in a way to which they are
> accustomed and that suits their learning style,
> media specialists need to know their audience.
> To communicate effectively with members of
> oral cultures, we need to communicate in ways
> appropriate for oral communicators. We also
> need to make good use of non-print media.
>
> A person from a print orientation might object,
> saying that the people need a book to look
> things up in, but . . . oral communicators don't

look things up; they retrieve them from their
memory. The print-oriented person is amazed
that an oral communicator can happily listen to
a tape repeatedly, day after day, and even more
amazed at how quickly he or she memorizes it.
In oral cultures people easily memorize large
portions of Scripture.

So how do people think and learn in oral
cultures? Oral communicators learn by hearing,
while print communicators learn by seeing
and reading. Oral communicators think
and talk about events, not words. They "use
stories of human action to store, organize, and
communicate much of what they know." They
learn by watching and imitating, by listening
and repeating. Memorizing is easy for them.
They memorize things handed down from
the past: proverbs, stories, sayings, and songs.
Print communicators, on the other hand, think
and talk about words, concepts and principles.
They learn by reading, studying, classifying,
comparing and analyzing. They are poor at
memorizing and need to look things up in
books and write them down in notebooks.[182]

Jesus was an oral communicator. He communicated
using parables, stories, visual images and miracles. Even
literate learners, such as the Pharisees and Teachers of the
Law, received the messages of Jesus loud and clear when he
challenged and confronted them through parables and stories.

There is great value in literate communicators being exposed to oral communication styles, because oral and visual communication is the easiest to retain. The sermons and messages I recall with the most clarity are those infused with stories.

As a literate print-based learner I have the option of learning through both styles; oral learners do not have this luxury. If we ignore the need of oral learners to receive God's Word through oral communication, we will not be able to effectively share the Gospel with them.

Providing the Bible on CD may be a good place to start communicating the truth of God's Word to oral learners, encouraging people to listen to the passages from God's Word and then come together to discuss the passage and apply it to everyday life.

Audio Bible

While appearing on a Christian TV talk show recently I met a fellow guest named Brian Hardin. I was captivated by Brian's story and how it uniquely demonstrates the simple but profound value of communicating to primary and secondary oral learners in an appropriate format.

In 2005, Brian was a successful music producer, graphic artist and photographer with more than 150 Christian music albums to his credit. But God had different plans for Brian's life. Using a financial crisis in Brian's business, God upturned Brian's world, bringing him to a point of brokenness and rededication. Realizing he had strayed a long way from God, Brian told God he was prepared to do anything for him. Amazingly, after months of "alone time" with God seeking his guidance, all God told Brian to do was read the Bible.

At the time Brian had been experimenting with podcasts[183] as a means to expand his business. Brian decided he would record himself reading the Bible every day and invite people to listen to his Bible reading by downloading it as a podcast. It was at this point that God began to miraculously bless Brian's obedience. Surprisingly, more than two hundred people downloaded the first podcast. Soon hundreds more people started downloading the podcasts, and then thousands, then tens of thousands, and finally millions! At the time of the writing of this book, after his reading the Bible "online" daily for 1,862 consecutive days, there have been more than 39 million downloads of Brian's daily Bible reading. Every day thousands more join Brian's *Daily Audio Bible* community from all over the world.

Brian has numerous stories of people whose lives have been transformed by hearing the daily reading of God's Word. A rapidly growing global community of "Bible listeners" has emerged, populated by people collectively praying for the advancement of God's Kingdom. One third of *Daily Audio Bible* listeners are from China.

Brian Hardin is impacting the world for Jesus, and all that he is doing is simply reading the Bible to people every day— communicating God's Word in a culturally relevant way. In the "bio" on his website Brian concludes, "I want to finish well and have ripples of my life going on for generations to follow. I want it to matter for the Kingdom of God that I was here."

Godly Servant-hearted Leadership

Servant-hearted self-sacrificing leadership accompanied by a personal integrity that is grounded in mutual accountability is common to all Kingdom-advancing movements of God. In

Mark 10:43–44 we are told by Jesus that "Whoever wants to become great among you must be your servant, and whoever wants to be first must be a slave of all." When leaders don't model a Jesus-style leadership—humility, generosity, love, compassion and selflessness—there will be no genuine Kingdom growth.

Character

Over the years I have come to realize that we have a tendency in Christian ministries and churches to focus more on competence than character. We are prone to appoint the "most capable" to strategic leadership roles, even though they may have obvious character flaws. In every case where I have made leadership appointments based upon competence—capabilities, talents and gifts—rather than character, I ended up having to deal with distracting personnel problems and ongoing, debilitating organizational issues that frustrated ministry and resulted in a misrepresentation of the person of Jesus and the values of his Kingdom. Now, whenever I appoint a leader, I look first at the prospects' character before even considering their competence:

- Do they practice lives of self-sacrifice and integrity?
- Are they humble and honest?
- Do they consistently, deliberately and willingly surround themselves with accountability partners and give others the authority to speak into their lives?
- Do they genuinely care about others, going out of their way to bless and serve them?
- Do they allow others to lead, sharing their leadership

responsibilities and empowering people to serve to their full capacity?

- Do they want the best for others and desire for those around them to excel in their unique areas of strength and giftedness?

- Do they live under the authority of God's Word and value prayer as a vital component of their walk with Jesus?

- How do they treat people who can do nothing for them?

- Do they live what they preach?

The Bible provides us with a comprehensive list of qualifications for leadership. In 1 Timothy and Titus we are told that a leader in the Church needs to be self-controlled, hospitable, able to teach, gentle, not violent, not quarrelsome, not a lover of money, not a recent convert, of good reputation with outsiders, not overbearing, not quick-tempered, good, upright, holy, disciplined, above reproach, blameless, husband of one wife, temperate, respectable, not given to drunkenness, sincere, tested, honest, able to manage their family well and a person who holds to the truth.[184] Almost all of these qualifications for leadership have to do with character and integrity. So, from a biblical perspective, character is the foundation upon which leadership is built and maintained. If we elevate giftedness, capability, popularity and perceived success above character in the selection of leaders, we are acting outside of the mandates of God's Word.

I can't stress enough how important godly leadership is

to effective Kingdom ministry and community. I would urge any who aspire to serve in positions of leadership to guard their integrity—to build around them the accountability and support structures that will ensure they remain true to the biblical prerequisites of Kingdom leadership. I urge any who are responsible for selecting and appointing leaders to thoroughly investigate the integrity and character of those they are considering for leadership roles. And I urge those who would serve under the leadership of a pastor, minister or leader in a Christian ministry to ascertain the character of their leader, to ensure they not only advocate for the values of the Kingdom but live by them.

Our ultimate leader is Jesus, but he appoints leaders within his Kingdom to serve and inspire others by modeling a life of humility, love, grace and self-sacrifice. Many may claim to be leaders, but only those who lead like Jesus are the ones we should follow. Paul was such a leader, and because of his integrity he could confidently say, "Follow my example, as I follow the example of Christ."[185] The only valid leaders in God's Kingdom are those who can stand alongside Paul and humbly but honestly declare their integrity as representatives of Jesus.

Calling

The second factor essential for leadership in a Kingdom movement is "calling." A clear sense of call from God motivates a person to make significant personal sacrifices and to persevere in the face of opposition, disappointments, lack of resources, failures and personal problems. If a person perceives a leadership position in the Kingdom as a "job" rather than a calling, then he does not belong in leadership. When a leader does not have a call to serve in a Kingdom endeavor, then as soon as things get tough, the most likely outcome will be departure from the leadership role or a readjustment or dismissal of God-given values and goals.

Having a sense of calling from God is not only important for leaders serving in his Kingdom, but for all followers of Jesus. In Galatians Paul shares his calling, "I want you to know, brothers, that the gospel I preached is not something that man made up. I did not receive it from any man, nor was I taught it; rather, I received it by revelation from Jesus Christ."[186] Then in 1 Corinthians 9 Paul explains how important this calling is to his ministry: "Yet when I preach the gospel, I cannot boast, for I am compelled to preach. Woe to me if I do not preach the gospel! If I preach voluntarily, I have a reward; if not voluntarily, I am simply discharging the trust committed to me."[187]

Too many Christians in the church today serve with a "volunteer mentality." The problem with doing something "voluntarily" is that the basis for service is our personal choice rather than a directive from Jesus. Paul says if we serve voluntarily—without a call—we legitimately expect a reward because we are choosing to serve "out of the goodness of our heart." The problem is when it is by our choice that we serve, we can also "choose" to stop serving when the going gets tough. When we do something voluntarily we are not obligated to a higher authority, we are only answerable to ourselves.

However, if we place ourselves under Jesus' authority, consult with him about what he wants us to do and where he wants us to serve, and we get clear instructions from him, then the choice is taken out of our hands. When we serve with a calling we cannot withdraw from that service just because things get difficult or we feel underappreciated, frustrated or discouraged. As Paul says, if we have a calling from Jesus, then woe to us if we don't do what he has called us to do.

Oswald Chambers said, "It is easier to serve God without a vision, easier to work without a call, because then you are not bothered with what God requires."[188]

Many in the Church today travel through life without ever seriously asking Jesus what he would like them to do with the life that supposedly belongs to him. This is either because they are ambivalent about Jesus and don't place a high priority on his input, or because they are afraid of what he will ask them to do. When you seriously seek a calling from God, he will direct you where to go and what to do; and what he asks of you will most likely be disruptive, demanding and costly. But the rewards of following a call far outweigh the costs. Aligning with God's purpose for your life brings unparalleled fulfillment and great joy as you see others blessed through your service.

Throughout our ministry life Jenny and I have had unequivocal calls from God to each of our ministry and leadership roles. There have been moments when facing obstacles, disappointments, opposition and personal attack that I have said to Jenny something like "I can't do this anymore," or "Why should we put up with this? Let's go somewhere else where we will be appreciated." But self-pity doesn't last long in the context of a call. The conclusion we always come to is "God has told us to do this and until he tells us otherwise we need to keep doing what we have been called to do—no matter what the cost."

Perseverance is required to serve in the Kingdom of God. Calling is the key to persevering; without a strong sense of calling we will have no incentive to persist. When addressing the Thessalonians Paul said: "Therefore, among God's churches we boast about your perseverance and faith in all the persecutions and trials you are enduring. All this is evidence that God's judgment is right, and as a result you will be counted worthy of the kingdom of God, for which you are suffering."[189] Our perseverance and faithfulness to Jesus' call is directly linked to our worthiness to serve in the Kingdom of God.

Competence

Although competence by itself, when not accompanied by godly character and calling, is an inadequate qualifier for leadership in the Kingdom, it is a necessary component to leading effectively in Kingdom endeavors. God distributes gifts, or competencies, to all in his Kingdom, and it is his intention that these gifts be used for the purpose they are given—to serve him and others.

In Romans 12 we are told:

> We have different gifts, according to the grace
> given us. If a man's gift is prophesying, let him
> use it in proportion to his faith. If it is serving,
> let him serve; if it is teaching, let him teach;
> if it is encouraging, let him encourage; if it is
> contributing to the needs of others, let him give
> generously; if it is leadership, let him govern
> diligently; if it is showing mercy, let him do it
> cheerfully.[190]

If someone is given a leadership gift, it is given so that the person can lead.

Many gifts are listed in God's Word[191] apart from the leadership gifts.[192] Not everyone is gifted for leadership, and therefore not all can be positional leaders. Being of impeccable character, while being indispensable to effective leadership in God's Kingdom, does not necessarily qualify someone for a leadership role; a leader also needs a call from God to the role and gifts that align with the calling. Appointing godly people who do not have leadership gifts to positions of leadership generally ends up with both them and those they lead becoming frustrated and disillusioned.

Using gifts for Kingdom purposes

Kingdom leadership requires the employment of leadership gifts in Kingdom pursuits. The express purpose of the gifts that God gives his people is that they be used to serve others, foster unity, promote maturity and overall build the capacity of the members of God's family to authentically express the character of Christ.[193]

Ultimately, how we use God-given talents and gifts depends upon our life allegiances. If our primary allegiance is to ourselves—our advancement, reputation, comfort, security, happiness—then we will employ our talents in self-serving pursuits. If our allegiance is to God, then we will use our gifts in sacrificial service for others and the advancement of God's Kingdom.

When godly character, specific calling and appropriate competence are evident in a leader, great things can be done for the Kingdom.

Sacrificial Service to Others

When we truly embrace Jesus, the values and passions of the Kingdom dominate our lives and we can't help but respond to the needs of others. Kingdom movements throughout history have transformed society as those who joined the movements responded to the call of Jesus to serve those around them.

The people who led the great awakenings and revivals of the past three hundred years were known for their devotion to God and love for others. They passionately pursued a life of purity and service, conveying their overwhelming love for others in their fervor for the gospel as well as their practical response to the needs of their "neighbors." Justice for the oppressed, food for the hungry, freeing of slaves, homes for orphans, schools for the uneducated, care for the poor—all these services were endemic to these great movements of God.

As noted in Chapter 4, the early church is a classic example of sacrificial service to others. We are told in Acts, "All the believers were together and had everything in common. Selling their possessions and goods, they gave to anyone as he had need."[194] If a community of believers claims to be part of the Kingdom of God, one of the evidences of the authenticity of this claim will be sacrificial giving and service to the needy.

The Centrality and Preeminence of Jesus

Common to all outstanding movements of God is the preeminence and sovereignty of Jesus.

Jesus is the only way

The Bible is very clear that there is only one way for people to have an eternal soul-saving relationship with God, and that is through Jesus:

> Salvation is found in no one else, for there is no other name under heaven given to men by which we must be saved. (Acts 4:12)

> But now a righteousness from God, apart from law, has been made known, to which the Law and the Prophets testify. This righteousness from God comes through faith in Jesus Christ to all who believe. There is no difference, for all have sinned and fall short of the glory of God, and are justified freely by his grace through the redemption that came by Christ Jesus. (Romans 3:21–24)

> Therefore, since we have been justified through faith, we have peace with God through our Lord Jesus Christ, through whom we have gained access by faith into this grace in which we now stand. (Romans 5:1–2)

> That if you confess with your mouth, "Jesus is Lord," and believe in your heart that God raised him from the dead, you will be saved. For it is with your heart that you believe and are justified, and it is with your mouth that you confess and are saved. (Romans 10:9–10)

Jesus himself claimed to be the only way for anyone to come to God and to have eternal life:

> I am the way and the truth and the life. No one comes to the Father except through me. (John 14:6)

> I am the resurrection and the life. He who believes in me will live, even though he dies; and whoever lives and believes in me will never die. (John 11:25–26)

Jesus didn't say he was "a way," he said he was "the way." The Bible is unequivocal in its teaching that Jesus is the only way of salvation; any digression from this tenet of faith is only possible through ignorance or outright rejection of biblical truth.

Evangelism would make no sense if there were many ways to God, because there would be little incentive or need to share Jesus with others. All the movements that have produced great harvests for the Kingdom have been populated by people who believed that Jesus is the only way to salvation and that those who don't know him are heading to a lost eternity.

The sovereignty of Jesus

Jesus claimed to be one with God. He said, "I and the Father are one."[195] The Jewish leaders knew exactly what Jesus meant when he said this, and they were so incensed that they tried to kill him. When Jesus questioned their murderous intent they replied, "We are stoning you for blasphemy, because you, a mere man, claim to be God."[196]

Another time the Jews tried to stone Jesus when he stated "I tell you the truth, before Abraham was born, I am!"[197] In this statement Jesus declared his eternal nature—his preexistence before time—an attribute only possessed by God. In using the term "I am" to describe himself, Jesus was identifying with the name God used in communicating with the people of Israel:

> Moses said to God, "Suppose I go to the Israelites and say to them, 'The God of your fathers has sent me to you,' and they ask me, 'What is his name?' Then what shall I tell them?" God said to Moses, "I AM WHO I AM This is what you are to say to the Israelites: 'I AM has sent me to you.'"[198]

The Bible states that Jesus is the creator of the world,[199] the sustainer of life,[200] worthy of worship[201] and our Lord and God.[202] Being in very essence God, Jesus warrants our devotion, adoration, worship and obedience. Jesus is Lord and Savior in any God-honoring movement.

Following Jesus

Believing in Jesus is not enough. Even if you accept God's Word as truth and believe in Jesus' identity and way of salvation, unless you follow him it will be an empty belief. As we have seen throughout this book, Jesus calls us to do more than simply believe in him, he calls us to follow him.

There are many who claim to believe in Jesus but their belief has little or no impact on their lives. The people who populated the great revivals and Kingdom movements that changed the world were sold out to Jesus. Jesus was preeminent in their lives and he radically changed them and the world around them. They not only believed in Jesus, but they "walked with Jesus daily," growing in their relationship with him and shining the light of his love and grace into the world.

"Let your light shine before men, that they may see your good deeds and praise your Father in heaven."[203]

CHAPTER 10

THE POWER OF THE KINGDOM

"The kingdom of heaven is like a mustard seed, which a man took and planted in his field. Though it is the smallest of all your seeds, yet when it grows, it is the largest of garden plants and becomes a tree, so that the birds of the air come and perch in its branches."
(Matthew 13:31–32)

Jose Carlos had a college education, a well-paying job and a promising career when God called him to serve as a youth pastor in a small church in Monterey, Mexico. Although the church didn't have enough money to fully support Jose Carlos, he willingly and enthusiastically took on the youth ministry role, supplementing his meager church income by cleaning offices and commercial buildings. Not long after he started in his role a team from Youth for Christ USA came to his city to build houses for the poor and conduct youth outreach programs in a community not far from Monterey. The team was looking for an interpreter, and after much pleading from the pastor of his church, Jose Carlos reluctantly agreed to take on the task. His two weeks with the team were life changing.

Throughout the day, as the team worked on the houses, many young people congregated around the building projects and interacted with the team members. In the evenings the team conducted outreach programs, which involved drama and music that creatively communicated the story of Jesus. Each day Jose Carlos was able to get to know more and more young people. One young man in particular stood out. He had a long fingernail on his little finger, which indicated he was a cocaine user. One day this young man arrived with a beaming smile. Jose Carlos noticed that he had cut off his long fingernail. When he asked the young man what had happened to him, he told Jose Carlos that he had decided to become a follower of Jesus, and now that he had Jesus in his life, he no longer needed drugs. Over the days that the team remained in this town, Jose Carlos saw a dramatic change in this young man's life. He started helping the team build houses and found ways to serve the poor. He shared his story with many others and encouraged them to follow Jesus as well.

Jose Carlos's experience with the Youth for Christ team gave him a vision for reaching the youth of his nation. In the short time he was with the young people of the town he had seen many lives transformed by the power of Jesus. He reasoned that if so much could be achieved for the Kingdom in just a few weeks, how much more could be done if he dedicated the rest of his life to sharing Jesus with young people? He talked to the leader of the team about the possibility of serving in the Youth for Christ ministry, and the team leader connected him with the Youth for Christ Pioneering Director for the Americas.

At the time Youth for Christ was looking for someone to pioneer a national ministry in Mexico. Jose Carlos was ideal for the role—a young leader in his mid-twenties with a strong sense of calling to youth ministry that was already being expressed in a life of sacrifice and service. After several meetings with the Pioneering Director Jose Carlos was appointed as the Coordinator of Youth for Christ Mexico.

Jose Carlos enthusiastically jumped into the ministry, recruiting other young people to help him establish youth service and outreach initiatives. He set up an extensive sports program for marginalized and at-risk young people. The ministry grew quickly and after six months there were around eight hundred young people involved in their outreach programs.

Keen to develop his leadership skills, Jose Carlos enrolled in the Youth for Christ young leader development program, which involved him attending a gathering of young leaders in South Africa. It was at this gathering that God challenged Jose Carlos to higher levels of sacrifice and service. During a discussion group with other young leaders from various nations that were hostile to Christians, Jose Carlos heard many stories of courage, boldness, faithfulness and persecution. Under heavy conviction of the Holy Spirit he left the small group and ran to the prayer room, fell on his knees and in tears confessed to God that he was "doing nothing" compared to these other young people. He declared that he was prepared to give everything to reach the youth of his nation.

Jose Carlos left South Africa with a renewed vision and passion for sharing Jesus with the young people of his nation. The first thing he did when he got back to Mexico was to meet with his fiancée, Sara, and tell her what had happened in South Africa. Their wedding was just a few months away. After praying together about Jose Carlos's experiences in

South Africa, they decided to postpone their wedding for two years and use the funds they had saved for the wedding ceremony to grow the ministry.

Jose Carlos handed over the ministry in Monterey to another young leader so he could focus on pioneering new ministry in other states across Mexico. Captivated by his passion, call and vision, many other young people joined Jose Carlos and his small team, and the ministry was established in a number of other cities across Mexico.

After two years Jose Carlos and Sara finally married. They were still living in Monterey and were able to get enough together for a deposit on a small home, which they lovingly renovated. As they prayed together each day they became increasingly aware that God was asking them to get prepared to move out of Monterey. Unsure of where God wanted them to go, they simply said to him they would go wherever he sent them. After several weeks of prayer they became more and more convinced of where it was God wanted them to move— the border town of Juarez.

Juarez is the most dangerous city in Mexico and one of the most dangerous cities in the world. It is controlled by drug cartels and is known as "murder city." Four cartels in the city are constantly battling for control. Thousands of people are killed each year, many of them innocent residents of the city who get caught in the violence. The cartels recruit and pay large sums of money to thirteen- and fourteen-year-old teenagers to murder people. They demand protection money from businesses, churches and schools and have murdered business owners, pastors and principals who have refused to pay.

When it was clear that God wanted Jose Carlos and Sara

to move to Juarez, Sara cried every night for three weeks. But they were obedient to the Lord and moved to Juarez to care for and share Jesus with young people. It took them some time to get anything going as they had no contacts or friends in the city. But they slowly started to connect with local believers and eventually recruited a team of young leaders, started some soccer clubs and service ministries and began connecting with young people.

It wasn't easy. Representatives from the local drug cartel visited them and warned them against doing anything with the young people in their cartel. After a brief visit to the United States they returned to find the front of their rented home literally torn off, with most of their furnishings, appliances and possessions stolen. They desperately missed family and friends and experienced great loneliness in the hostile and unfriendly environment. But their faithfulness was rewarded and their ministry grew, not only in Juarez but across the nation. Many young people came to Jesus. Other young followers of Jesus joined the Youth for Christ ministry and obediently and sacrificially followed the call of Jesus to give everything for him and his Kingdom.

In a two-year period, under the leadership of Jose Carlos and Sara, the Youth for Christ ministry was established in eight states of Mexico. In the second year Jose Carlos and his ever-expanding team ministered to more than twenty thousand young people. Through sacrifice and faithfulness the seed of the Kingdom that was sown in the life of Jose Carlos in that little town on the outskirts of Monterey had grown and blossomed and produced much fruit.

The Cost of the Kingdom

In Matthew 13 Jesus said, "The kingdom of heaven is like treasure hidden in a field. When a man found it, he hid it again, and then in his joy went and sold all he had and bought that field. Again, the kingdom of heaven is like a merchant looking for fine pearls. When he found one of great value, he went away and sold everything he had and bought it."[204]

In Luke 14:33 Jesus stated, "Any of you who does not give up everything he has cannot be my disciple." And in Mark 8:34–35 Jesus said, "If anyone would come after me, he must deny himself and take up his cross and follow me. For whoever wants to save his life will lose it, but whoever loses his life for me and for the gospel will save it."

The process of becoming a follower of Jesus is sometimes described as "giving your life to Jesus." This is an apt descriptor, because following Jesus requires that we give up everything for him—possessions, family, career, ambitions, wealth and ultimately, our life.

When Jesus encountered the rich young ruler he quickly honed in on the one thing that was more precious to him than his place in the Kingdom. Jesus said to him, "Go, sell everything you have and give to the poor, and you will have treasure in heaven. Then come, follow me."[205] We are told that the young man "went away sad, because he had great wealth."[206] As this man walked away dejected Jesus said to his disciples, "How hard it is for the rich to enter the kingdom of God!"[207]

Today, those of us who live in developed nations are the rich Jesus referred to. According to the World Bank Development Research Group, "If your income is more than

$25,000 per year, you are wealthier than approximately 90 percent of the world's population! If you make $50,000 per year, you are wealthier than 99 percent of the world."[208] How much of our wealth are we prepared to give up for Jesus?

For the Kingdom to come in the Church and in the world it must first come in us; and for the Kingdom of God to come in us we need to give up everything for the Kingdom. When we give our lives to Jesus he asks us to give up the "ownership" of our money, possessions and relationships. In our life transaction with Jesus everything becomes his and we become stewards of the things we once thought we owned. If Jesus needs our money to establish his Kingdom, or our house, our car or even our life, he has the right to demand them from us, because they belong to him.

In the story of Helen in Chapter 4, when I turned up to that church family's home and asked them to look after Helen, from my somewhat naive perspective, I reasoned that Helen needed a place to stay and this family had room in their home, their home belonged to Jesus, and so I was simply asking them to let Helen stay in Jesus' house.

Where do we draw the line for what Jesus has access to in our lives? What are we prepared to make available to him and his Kingdom? Jose Carlos and Sara put Jesus in charge of everything. When Jesus needed their marriage, they willing gave that up and postponed their wedding, using the resources they had saved for the advancement of the Kingdom. When they were asked for their home and comfort, once again Jose Carlos and Sara recognized the ownership of Jesus and gave up their home for him and his Kingdom.

Radical Living

David Platt has been labeled "the youngest megachurch pastor in history."[209] At the age of twenty-seven Platt was appointed as senior pastor of The Church at Brook Hills in Birmingham, Alabama. Over a five year period the church grew rapidly into "megachurch" proportions, but not on the all-too-common diet of prosperity, entertainment and sugar-coated Christianity. Platt preaches and practices a radical, self-sacrificing, Kingdom-focused message that demands much from those in his church community. In his book *Radical: Taking Back Your Faith from the American Dream*, Platt challenges the false values of the American church and calls people to a life of simplicity, biblical truth, self-denial and mission. In the first chapter of his book, where he focuses on what "radical abandonment" to Jesus means, he states:

> We are giving in to the dangerous temptation
> to take Jesus of the Bible and twist him into
> a version of Jesus with whom we are more
> comfortable, a nice, middle-class, American
> Jesus. A Jesus who doesn't mind materialism and
> who would never call us to give away everything
> we have.[210]

Platt goes on in his book to describe the radical all-or-nothing life that Jesus requires us to live if we would follow him. He presents Jesus and his Kingdom as "something worth losing everything for" and asks people to consider "a proper response" to the gospel, stating, "Surely more than praying a prayer is involved. Surely more than religious attendance is warranted. Surely this gospel invokes unconditional surrender of all that we are and all that we have to all that he is."[211]

Platt practices what he preaches. He downsized to a smaller home and reduced his spending so that he could give more to missions and the needy. He encourages his congregants to consider what God is asking them to give up, to commit a percentage of their time to missions, to foster and adopt homeless and orphaned children, to engage in long-term extensive Bible study, and to move into and serve poor communities.

Under Platt's leadership, budgeted expenses of Brook Hills were cut 18 percent, impacting many of the entertainment programs and comforts of the church, while the general mission giving was increased 24 percent, on top of already designated mission giving of over one million dollars.[212] He even explored the possibility of the church selling its multi-million-dollar campus and giving the money to the poor.[213]

In the sermon series where he first started to explore radical living for Jesus, Platt stated:

> What if there really were billions of people on this planet who are headed to an eternal hell, and millions of them that haven't heard the name of Jesus? And what if there were unprecedented numbers of suffering people on this planet? And what if God decided to give his people on this side unprecedented wealth to make a difference among the lost and the poor? What if that is exactly what he has done?[214]

Platt doesn't direct what his church members should give of their money or themselves. He encourages his church to "dig deeper into God's Word and focus on knowing Christ, hearing from him, and obeying him."²¹⁵ He tells his own story, provides opportunity for people to study and apply God's Word, encourages involvement in ministry and mission, and models generous and wise giving; but he leaves it up to Jesus to challenge and direct people in their Kingdom response.

Platt and the Brook Hills church community aren't perfect, but they are a great example of what is possible when godly leaders foster and encourage a radical abandonment to Jesus, devotion to and application of God's Word, concerted prayer, sacrificial giving, passion for the lost, and practical service to the poor and needy. The Kingdom has come at The Church at Brook Hills in Birmingham, Alabama, and now it is coming in the lives of many in the Birmingham community and beyond, to many other places in the world where Brook Hills serves.

Available

Not long after Jenny and I were married someone gave us a small plaque which has hung on the wall of every home we have lived in; it reads, "God never asks about our ability or our inability; but about our availability." Since receiving that plaque, Jenny and I have had many moments of calling wherein God has called us to do something that is way beyond our abilities and that has often involved significant sacrifice and disruption to our life. Every time this has happened, before God told us what he wanted us to do, he first asked us to be available.

Being part of God's Kingdom means totally abandoning yourself to Jesus' will and way and making yourself available to him to use however he chooses—to go wherever he wishes to send you, to give whatever he asks you to give, and to serve whomever he wants you to serve.

In his challenging book *Experiencing God* Henry Blackaby says:

> God is wanting to reveal Himself to a watching world. He does not call you to get involved just so people can see what you can do. He calls you to an assignment that you cannot do without Him. The assignment will have God-sized dimensions. . . . I have come to the place in my life that, if the assignment I sense God is giving me is something that I know I can handle, I know it probably is not from God. The kind of assignments God gives in the Bible are always God-sized. They are always beyond what people can do because He wants to demonstrate His nature, His strength, His provision, and His kindness to His people and to a watching world. That is the only way the world will come to know Him.[216]

God calls us all to be available to him. Are you prepared to say to the Lord, "I am available; I totally surrender my life to you; do whatever you want with me to grow your Kingdom"? When we do this God can and will use us to do great things for him and his Kingdom.

The Power of the Kingdom

When the Kingdom comes in the world, it has the potential to have an enormous and ever-expanding impact.

Sowing the seeds of the Kingdom in one life has the power to transform whole communities. Many of the young people to whom I have introduced Jesus over the years have gone on to share their experience of the Kingdom with others. Whole families, communities, churches, and in some cases nations have been impacted through the sowing of the seeds of the Kingdom in these young people's lives.

You may ask yourself, "What difference can I make?" "Is my sacrifice and dedication to God going to change anything?" But God doesn't call us to worry about the results of serving him; he simply calls us to be faithful. What we know from the words of Jesus is that when we invest ourselves in the establishment of God's Kingdom on this earth, he will take that investment and multiply it beyond our comprehension.

May God's Kingdom come; may his will be done, on earth as it is in heaven.

ENDNOTES

1   Name changed to protect privacy
2   James 2:15–17
3   Matthew 6:9–13; Luke 11:2–4
4   Matthew 3:2
5   Luke 18:22
6   Matthew 4:19–22
7   Matthew 19:27
8   This story is based upon a true story—particularly the account of Paul being likened to Jesus—but names have been changed and some details added.
9   Philippians 2:3–8
10 Romans 7:14–24
11 Revelation 3:16 (The word used is sometimes translated "spit" but the literal translation is "vomit.")
12 Revelation 3:15
13 Matthew 23:15, 23; Mark 2:27; Luke 11:46, 52
14 WordWeb
15 Matthew 23:23
16 Matthew 23:13–15
17 Luke 17:20
18 Romans 6:14
19 2 Corinthians 3:6; Galatians 5:18
20 Philip Yancey, *What's So Amazing About Grace* (Grand Rapids: Zondervan Publishing House, 1997), 45.
21 Romans 3:21–24, 28
22 1 John 2:6
23 Luke 6:45
24 Matthew 7:15–20
25 Galatians 5:22–23
26 Dallas Willard, "Spiritual Formation: What It Is, and How It Is Done," Dallas Willard.org.
27 Romans 12:2
28 This explanation of prayer and intimacy with Jesus is taken from my book, *The Next Wave* (Colorado Springs: NavPress, 2007).
29 *Zondervan NIV Bible Commentary* (Grand Rapids: Zondervan Publishing House, 2002).
30 *Asbury Bible Commentary* (Grand Rapids: Zondervan Publishing House, 2002).
31 Romans 12:1–2
32 Micah 6:6–8
33 John 1:1; Revelation 19:3
34 Matthew, Mark, Luke and John
35 James 1:23–24
36 John 14:6
37 John 10:10
38 Matthew 5:45
39 Matthew 5:9; Luke 6:35
40 Galatians 3:26
41 Galatians 4:5
42 John 12:21 (KJV)
43 2 Kings 6 & 7
44 2 Kings 7:6
45 2 Kings 7:9
46 http://www.youtube.com/watch?v=VdvES4_MJ5Y
47 K.S. Wang, "Celebrity Drive: Penn Jillette, Magician, Comedian, Host, Author," *Motor Trend* (June 1, 2009).
48 2 Corinthians 5:14–15
49 Matthew 10:7; Mark 13:10; 16:15
50 1 Corinthians 3:6–7
51 Acts 12:24; Acts 13:49; Acts 19:20; 2 Thessalonians 3:1
52 John 4:7–26
53 John 3:1–21
54 1 Corinthians 9:19–23
55 Matthew 4:23; 24:14; Mark 9:35; 13:10
56 Luke 4:43
57 Matthew 28:18–20
58 Ephesians 5:16; Colossians 4:5–6
59 Matthew 22:39
60 Mark 16:15
61 Matthew 28:19–20
62 Matthew 28:19–20
63 Acts 2:22–24, 32
64 Mark 12:30–31
65 Rowland Croucher, "Church Attendance in Australia," *John Mark Ministries* online magazine, 10 April 2006; Noelle Knox, "Religion Takes a Back Seat in Western Europe," *USA Today* 11 August 2005.
66 Brian Fulthrop, "Church Attendance Is Dropping Amongst Anglicans-Episcopalians," *New Epistles* online magazine, 15 September 2009.
67 David Wraight, *The Next Wave* (Colorado Springs: NavPress, 2007), 131–32.
68 King James Version
69 David Kinnaman & Gabe Lyons, *unChristian* (Grand Rapids: Baker Books, 2007), 41.

70 Kinnaman & Lyons, *unChristian*, 181.

71 Kinnaman & Lyons, *unChristian*, 219.

72 Electa Draper, "1 in 4 Americans Can't Think of Recent Positive Contribution by Christians," *Denver Post*, 26 October 2010.

73 Matthew 11:19

74 Matthew 13:31–33

75 Lana Gates, "Little Acts of Kindness Can Make a Big Difference," *Phoenix Examiner*, 9 February 2009.

76 Matthew 5:16

77 Ephesians 3:9

78 Ephesians 3:3–4

79 Ephesians 3:6

80 Acts 16:17; 18:25–26; 19:9, 23; 22:4; 24:14, 22

81 John 14:6

82 Acts 2:1–13

83 Galatians 2:14

84 Steve Addison, *Movements that Change the World* (Smyrna: Missional Press, 2009), 27.

85 Ibid., 28.

86 Ibid., 64–65.

87 Matthew 15:19

88 John 3:1–10

89 John 4:1–26

90 John 8:2-11

91 Not her real name. This story is based on a true story of a girl who came to Dhaka seeking work and ended up in prostitution, gave birth to a child and eventually died on the streets. The description of her death and the response of the people who passed by her body is factual.

92 Not his real name

93 Psalm 116:5

94 Psalm 145:9

95 2 Corinthians 1:3

96 Richard Stearns, *The Hole in Our Gospel* (Nashville: Thomas Nelson, 2009), 249.

97 Mark 10:17–31

98 Matthew 13:31–32

99 Not his real name

100 Isaiah 1:10–17

101 About 25 miles

102 Matthew 5:16; 24:14

103 Galatians 5:22–23

104 Huma Khan, "Child Sex Trafficking Growing in the U.S.", *ABC News*, Washington, (May 5, 2010)

105 Wikipedia, "Human Trafficking"

106 Isaiah 1:11-17

107 Amos 2:6–7, 13

108 Luke 11:42

109 Sarah Eekhoff Zylstra, "Boarding Bust," *Christianity Today*, January 2011.

110 Leviticus 19:15; Deuteronomy 1:17; Proverbs 24:23; James 2:1, 9

111 Amos 5:24

112 Name changed for privacy—this story is based on a true story of people being served by the Mobile Medical Clinic but the names and some of the details have been changed to protect the privacy of those receiving the medical care.

113 Pseudonym

114 There are around 46 million people in the United States who don't have medical insurance and in most cases have to personally pay the full costs of a visit to a doctor or any medical procedure.

115 Luke 10:25–37

116 Ezekiel 34:2–4

117 Richard Stearns, *The Hole in our Gospel* (Nashville: Thomas Nelson, 2009), 141.

118 Ibid., 142.

119 Matthew 10:1; Luke 9:6; Acts 3:6–8; 5:15–16; 8:6–8; 14:8–10; 28:7–9

120 1 Corinthians 12:9, 28, 30

121 James 5:14–15

122 Hebrews 13:8

123 Matthew 10:1

124 Acts 4:10; 14:8–15

125 Job 30:16, 27

126 Job 36:15

127 Psalm 23:3, 4, 6

128 1 Kings 19:4

129 1 Kings 19:12–13

130 1 Kings 19:18

131 John 8:3–11

132 John 4:39–42

133 Johnny's story is a real life story from Burundi. Some of the details of his parent's death are constructed from the little information we have from Johnny as well as experiences common to many orphaned young people in Burundi. Johnny was forced to eat his father's body to survive.

134 Matthew 15:32

135 Matthew 25:35

136 "World Hunger and Poverty
    Facts and Statistics 2010", www.
    worldhunger.org
137 According to a report by the United
    Nations Food and Agriculture
    Organization, as reported in
    "World Hunger and Poverty
    Facts and Statistics 2010", www.
    worldhunger.org
138 Proverbs 23:2
139 1 Corinthians 11:18–22
140 Matthew 23:25
141 "Water Facts"; www.water.org
142 "Diarhhoea: Why Children Are
    Still Dying and What Can Be
    Done," UNICEF; WHO 2009
143 Mark 10:5-9
144 Therese J. Borchard, "Find
    Emotional Peace After
    Divorce,"http://www.beliefnet.
    com/Health/Emotional-Health/
    Depression/12-Depression-
    Busters-for-Divorce.aspx
145 Genesis 2:18
146 Genesis 1:27; 2:22–24
147 Genesis 2:24; Mark 10:7–9
148 George Barna, "Born Again
    Christians Just As Likely to
    Divorce As Are Non-Christians,"
    The Barna Update, The Barna
    Group, September 2004.
149 Ken Camp, "Baptist Divorce Rate
    Higher than Average," *The Baptist
    Standard*, 12 January 2000.
150 Glenn Stanton, "First Person: The
    Christian divorce rate myth (what
    you've heard is wrong)," *Baptist
    Press*, March 16, 2011
151 Amy Desai, "Is There Hope for My
    Marriage", www.focusonthefamily.
    com.
152 A legal contract that details
    allocation of assets and finances in
    the event of marriage separation or
    divorce.
153 Song of Solomon 8:7 (NLT)
154 1 Corinthians 13
155 John 4:14
156 David Garrison, *Church Planting
    Movements: How God is Redeeming
    a Lost World* (Bangalore, India:
    WIGTake Resources, 2004).
157 Ibid., 172.
158 Steve Addison, *Movements that
    Changed the World* (Smyrna:
    Missional Press, 2009), 22–24.
159 James 5:17–18
160 Ephesians 3:20
161 Luke 9:23
162 Matthew 19:26
163 Mark 9:29
164 Ephesians 6:18
165 Matthew 18:19–20
166 Barry Hankins, *The Second
    Great Awakening and the
    Transcendentalists* (Westport,
    Conn.: Greenwood Press, 2004),
    137.
167 "Repentance," *NIV Bible Dictionary*
    (Grand Rapids, Mich.: Zondervan ,
    1999).
168 2 Peter 3:9
169 2 Corinthians 5:14–15
170 1 Corinthians 9:16
171 Garrison, *Church Planting
    Movements*, 182.
172 Barna Research Online,
    "Religious Beliefs Vary Widely by
    Denomination,"www.barna.org, 25
    June 2001.
173 Barna Research Online,
    "Discipleship Insights Revealed in
    New Book by George Barna," www.
    barna.org, 28 November 2000.
174 Russell Ash, *The Top 10 of
    Everything (New York: DK
    Publishers, 1996)*, 112–13.
175 2 Timothy 3:16–17
176 2 Peter 1:20–21
177 Matthew 21:42; 22:29; Mark 12:10,
    24; John 5:39; 7:38; 10:35; 13:18
178 John 10:35
179 Matthew 26:54; Mark 14:49; Luke
    4:21; 24:27, 32
180 John 2:22; Acts 1:16; 8:35; 18:28;
    Romans 1:2; 4:3; 9:17; 10:11; 15:4;
    1 Corinthians 15:3–4; Galatians
    3:8, 16, 22; 1 Timothy 4:13; 2
    Timothy 3:5, 16; James 2:8; 4:5–6;
    1 Peter 2:6; 2 Peter 1:20; 3:16
181 Acts 17:11
182 Rick Brown, "Communicating
    God's Message in Oral Cultures",
    *International Journal of Frontier
    Missions*, (Fall 2004), p. 27
183 A podcast (or non-streamed
    webcast) is a series of digital
    media files (either audio or video)
    that are released episodically and
    often downloaded through web
    syndication.
184 1 Timothy 3:2-10; Titus 1:6-9
185 1 Corinthians 11:1
186 Galatians 1:11–12

187   1 Corinthians 9:16–17
188   Oswald Chambers, *My Utmost for
      His Highest* (Uhrichsville, OH:
      Barbour Publishing, 1963), March
      4th
189   2 Thessalonians 1:4–5
190   Romans 12:6–8
191   Romans 12:6–8; 1 Corinthians
      12:1–11; Ephesians 4:11–16
192   prophecy, teaching, exhortation and
      evangelism
193   Ephesians 4:11–13
194   Acts 2:44–45
195   John 10:30
196   See John 10:33
197   John 8:58
198   Exodus 3:13–15
199   Colossians 1:16
200   Colossians 1:17
201   Romans 14:11; Philippians 2:10–
      11; Revelation 5:12
202   John 1:1; 20:28
203   Matthew 5:16

204   Matthew 13:44–46
205   Mark 10:21
206   Mark 10:22
207   Mark 10:23
208   Richard Stearns, *The Hole in our
      Gospel* (Nashville: Thomas Nelson,
      2009), 215.
209   David Platt, *Radical: Taking Back
      Your Faith from the American Dream*
      (Colorado Springs: Multnomah
      Books, 2010),. 1.
210   Ibid., 13.
211   Ibid., 37.
212   Robby Butler, "Going Radical,",
      Mission Frontiers (November-
      December, 2010), 7.
213   Ibid., 6.
214   Ibid., 8.
215   Ibid.
216   Henry Blackaby, *Experiencing God:
      Knowing and Doing the Will of God*
      (Nashville: LifeWay Press, 1998),
      220.